WINNING THE DEAL

MASTERING NEGOTIATION STYLES TO GROW YOUR ADVANTAGE

JIM SCHLECKSER
ONYI ODUNUKWE

POTOMAC RIVER
IMPRINTS

Published by Potomac River Press
P.O. Box 60602
Potomac, MD 20859

Book design by Draft Lab LLC.

Cover image—gold gradient background: © Amjad Ali 2 / Shutterstock.com

Paperback ISBN: 978-1-7350044-3-3
Ebook ISBN: 978-1-7350044-4-0

Printed in the United States of America
First edition

CONTENTS

TWO STYLES, ONE GOAL: A PRACTICAL PLAYBOOK FOR GETTING BETTER DEALS

NEGOTIATION ISN'T RESERVED FOR high-powered CEOs or hostage negotiators. It's for anyone who wants to get better outcomes in business and in life—whether you're closing on a property, buying a company, hiring talent, asking for a raise, or simply deciding who takes out the trash. The problem is that most people either avoid negotiation altogether or they wing it.

We wrote this book to help you improve.

But this isn't a lecture. It's a conversation, a contrast, a collision between two experienced negotiators—one strategic and collaborative, the other bold and unapologetically aggressive—who often take different routes to reach the same goal: the best possible deal.

MEET YOUR NEGOTIATORS

Jim Schleckser is a CEO advisor and seasoned strategist. He focuses on long-term success, builds trust, and rarely raises his voice. His approach is based on logic, patience, and preparation. He has negotiated hundreds of business contracts over his career.

Onyi Odunukwe is a commercial real estate investor, franchise owner, and dealmaker who has negotiated over 100 transactions. His approach? Make the pie bigger, not fight over slices. While others see negotiation as a tug-of-war, Onyi engineers deals where everyone walks away with more than they imagined—often by structuring creative solutions that unlock value others don't see. His secret: patience, perspective, and the willingness to walk away until the deal makes sense for all parties.

We don't always see eye to eye, and that's the point. There's no universal method for negotiations. What works in a corporate merger might not succeed in a real estate deal. What gets the job done in a salary discussion could fail in a joint venture. Different styles, different tools, same goal: a better deal.

Here's an example:

REAL LIFE NEGOTIATION—JIM: A few years ago, I received a package in the mail—no return address, just a large manila envelope. Inside? Confidential data from our biggest competitor. Customer lists. Pricing. Sales forecasts. Pure gold. And completely unethical to use.

I resealed it, sent it straight to the competitor's CEO, and gave him a call. Five years later, we finally met face-to-face. He shook my hand and told his colleague, "This guy? One of the ethical ones."

A year later, I bought his company. Not because I cut corners, but because I established trust. That trust and openness became the foundation of an excellent business arrangement for both parties.

REAL LIFE NEGOTIATION—ONYI: I once purchased a $2.8 million building with no cash out of pocket—and solved a major problem for the seller in the process. He was underwater on the property and facing a potential loss.

Instead of grinding him down, I offered him full price, which cleared his underwater loan, and structured financing at 0% interest so he kept equity in the deal. He signed an above-market lease because he wanted to stay in the building and the terms worked for his business.

Two years later, the building was valued at over $5 million. That's what happens when you focus on solving problems instead of "winning" negotiations. The best deals aren't extracted—they're engineered.

WHAT YOU'LL LEARN

We aim to provide you with a toolkit—not a script. Our aim is for you to leave this book more confident, capable, and better prepared to think strategically, adapt tactically, and succeed with integrity.

Each chapter in this book is a step in the full lifecycle of a deal. We don't just teach you what to say at the table—we walk you through the mindset, strategy, pressure points, recovery moments, and follow-up that shape successful negotiations from start to finish.

Here's how the book breaks down:

- **Chapter 1: Negotiation Philosophies—Which One Fits You?:** Learn the major schools of negotiation thought and discover which style best fits your natural instincts—and when to adapt.

- **Chapter 2: Before the Deal—Win It Before You Begin:** Everything necessary happens before the first handshake. This chapter shows you how to prepare, define your walkaway point, and develop a three-step reaction matrix.

- **Chapter 3: Tactics for a Successful Negotiation:** From anchoring and silence to humor and framing, you'll learn the most effective tools to use in real time—plus how to read the room and adjust on the fly.

- **Chapter 4: Negotiation Tactics to Avoid:** A savvy negotiator knows what not to do. We'll walk you through common pitfalls—like "nibbling," overplaying your hand, or chasing perfection—and show how to avoid sabotaging your own deals.

- **Chapter 5: Closing the Deal: Negotiation Tactics in Action:** Closing the deal isn't the end—it's the beginning of ensuring the agreement is implemented smoothly, protected legally, and structured for long-term success through clear documentation, competent legal counsel, and proactive relationship management.

- **Chapter 6: After the Negotiation:** What happens after the contract is signed? A lot. Discover how to follow through, prevent post-deal breakdowns, and cultivate momentum for the next opportunity.

WHY WE WROTE THIS BOOK

Because we've all seen the costs of poor negotiation—money left on the table, strained relationships, damaged reputations, or deals falling through. And we've also witnessed how a well-timed question, a thoughtful pause, or a creative term sheet can completely change the game.

Whether you're a seasoned pro or negotiating your first deal, this book serves as your field guide. It's not about winning at all costs. It's about achieving what matters, walking away confidently, and building a career where people want to negotiate with you again.

Let's get to work.

NEGOTIATION PHILOSOPHIES—WHICH ONE FITS YOU?

NEGOTIATION ISN'T ONE-SIZE-FITS-ALL. DIFFERENT situations need different approaches. What works in a corporate boardroom might not work in a real estate deal—or during a salary negotiation. In this chapter, we'll look at various established negotiation strategies, explain how they work in real-life situations, and share insights and stories from both of us—Jim and Onyi—about how we've used (or reacted to) each in real deals.

Before we dive into the deep analysis, take a look at the quick comparison of the schools of thought shown in the table.

Now, let's explore each of these philosophies in more detail and share some of our insights on when they work best and when they don't.

Negotiation Schools of Thought

School/Style	Key Traits	When to Use It	Jim's Take	Onyi's Take
Harvard (Principled)	Win-win, focus on interests, objective criteria	When trust matters, long-term deals	My go-to. It builds durable relationships.	Great when you have the upper hand.
Yale (Trust-Based)	Assertive yet empathetic, builds rapport	Ongoing partnerships, sensitive deals	Strong for team or talent negotiations.	Too soft if stakes are high.
Stanford (Adaptive)	Flexible, creative, context-driven	Fast-changing or ambiguous situations	Smart for complex, evolving negotiations.	Good—if you're the one setting the pace.
MIT (Analytical)	Data-focused, logical, systems-thinking	Tech, finance, and high-stakes deals	Great if you have the numbers.	Just don't forget the human element.
Chris Voss (FBI)	Empathy, mirroring, tactical silence	Emotional, high-pressure environments	Tactical empathy is powerful.	Silence and leverage—I'm all in.
Winner Takes All	Aggressive, zero-sum	Short-term, transactional deals	High risk, low relationship.	Fun—but only if you're holding aces.
Lose-Lose (Our Pick)	Mutual sacrifice for mutual gain	Complex deals with misaligned priorities	It's not weakness—it's strategy.	Give a little, get a lot—if you're smart.

THE HARVARD APPROACH: PRINCIPLED NEGOTIATION

The Harvard Negotiation philosophy, often referred to as the "principled negotiation" approach, is about finding solutions that benefit everyone involved. Instead of focusing on beating the other side or just splitting the difference, this method encourages both parties to collaborate and seek a mutually beneficial outcome:

1. **Separate People from the Problem:** Keep emotions out of the negotiation. Concentrate on resolving the issue, not criticizing the person.

2. **Focus on Interests, Not Positions:** Instead of sticking to your position (like "I want a higher salary"), identify the underlying reasons (your interest might be "I need enough money to cover my expenses"). This approach enables you to find innovative solutions that meet the needs of both parties.

3. **Invent Options for Mutual Gain:** Brainstorm multiple solutions to create choices and think creatively about ways both sides can succeed.

4. **Use Objective Criteria:** Rely on facts and standards, such as market value or legal precedents, instead of opinions or power struggles.

The Harvard style promotes collaboration and fairness, with the goal that everyone feels like they've gained something and there's no "winner" or "loser." It's an intelligent way to maintain good business relationships while getting your needs met.

JIM'S PERSPECTIVE: This is my preferred default style. It promotes mutual respect and lays the groundwork for long-term relationships. When I returned a confidential packet from a competitor and later bought their company, that was Harvard-style trust-building in action. Ultimately, the best deal isn't in hardline negotiations as those deals are unstable. A deep understanding of both parties to find a creative solution can build a lasting and stable relationship.

ONYI'S TAKE: Win-win is fine—it's table stakes. But honestly? It's boring. When you walk away from a win-win deal, you can't help but wonder: did we leave opportunity on the table?

That's why I don't stop at win-win. I go for win-MORE. Instead of splitting value fairly, I look for ways to create value that wouldn't exist otherwise. The $2.8M building deal I described in the last chapter? A win-win would've been negotiating a fair price, shaking hands, moving on. Instead, I structured 0% financing, an above-market lease, and cleared his debt—he got more relief than he imagined, I got the property with zero down, and two years later it's worth more than $5 million. That's not splitting a pie. That's baking a bigger one.

THE YALE SCHOOL

The Yale School of Negotiation is also about working together to find the best solution, but it focuses more on building trust and relationships while remaining firm about goals. It's less about the process and more about the people and the long-term connection you're creating.

1. **Build Trust:** The idea is to establish trust with the other side. They'll likely be open to negotiation and compromise if they trust you. Building a solid relationship matters just as much as getting to the result.

2. **Be Assertive and Fair:** If you want to maintain that relationship, you also need to be clear and assertive about what you need. Don't just roll over and agree to something that doesn't work for you—stand your ground but do it fairly and respectfully.

3. **Focus on Long-Term Gains:** The Yale philosophy encourages looking beyond the immediate deal. Instead, consider how this negotiation can help build a longer, more beneficial relationship.

4. **Manage Emotions:** Keep your cool. Stay calm and rational even if the negotiation gets tough. You want to maintain a positive atmosphere and avoid letting emotions ruin progress.

In short, the Yale approach mixes firmness with friendliness. It's about ensuring that both sides are satisfied while setting the stage for future deals. Trust, fairness, and long-term thinking are key here.

JIM'S PERSPECTIVE: This framework works well when interacting repeatedly with people such as board members or partners. Building trust can result in unexpected benefits over time. I find emotions the hardest part to manage in negotiations and some people cannot manage theirs. My rational and calm approach sometimes chills the room, but other times, we need to take a break to let the other party cool down.

ONYI'S TAKE: Building trust is essential, but the best way to build respect isn't by being agreeable, it's by being willing to walk away.

I've learned to show people I'm looking out for them, even when they can't see it yet. When I make a fair offer and someone pushes for unreasonable terms, I don't cave to preserve the relationship. I walk—but I leave them with dignity. No pressure, no hard feelings. Just: "I understand. Here's my offer when you're ready."

You know what happens? They come back. Sometimes months later, sometimes years later—often with worse options than what I originally offered. That's when they realize I wasn't playing games. I was just designing deals that actually made sense.

But here's the thing: yesterday's price isn't today's price. By being patient and principled, you create leverage. Not because you're punishing them, but because you've proven you're a principled negotiator worth working with. Respect comes from integrity, not from saying yes.

STANFORD SCHOOL OF NEGOTIATING

The Stanford School of Negotiation highlights the importance of flexibility and adaptability, combining strategy and creativity to achieve the best results. It's all about recognizing that each negotiation is different and being comfortable adjusting your approach based on the situation and the people involved.

1. **Stay strategically adaptable:** There's no "one size fits all" in negotiations. You need to be prepared to adjust your tactics according to the situation. Some cases might require you to be firm, while others need more cooperation. It's about understanding the environment and knowing when to adjust your approach.

2. **Focus on Collaboration:** Like other negotiation philosophies, Stanford encourages parties to work together rather than trying to "beat" one another. They believe that collaboration can often lead to a better deal for everyone.

3. **Get Creative:** Stanford promotes innovative problem-solving. Instead of relying on traditional negotiation methods, they recommend thinking outside the

box to find solutions that may not be immediately obvious.

4. **Understand Power Dynamics:** The Stanford approach stresses awareness of the authority balance in any negotiation. If you're in a stronger position, use it wisely—but if the other side holds more power, you need to find ways to negotiate without conceding too much.

In summary, the Stanford philosophy emphasizes being adaptable and innovative while prioritizing collaboration. It teaches you to adjust to the situation, leverage your strengths, and find ways to work together for a mutually beneficial outcome.

JIM'S PERSPECTIVE: This mindset is highly effective for complex or fast-changing deals. You adjust as the deal develops, especially when new information appears. I love that element of creativity in this model. That creativity comes from spending time understanding the other party and craft a solution that works.

ONYI'S TAKE: Adaptability is about adjusting your approach based on what the other party actually needs.

I once bought a property in Addison, Texas where one tenant was paying far below market rate. The obvious move? Raise his rent or kick him out. But I sat down with him first to understand his situation. Turns out, he didn't need to stay in my building—he needed an affordable space for his business.

So I adapted. I used my commercial real estate brokerage to find him a better location at a rent rate lower than what he would've paid if I'd let him stay. His business wasn't interrupted. He saved money. I brought in a market-rate tenant.

That's strategic adaptability: not forcing one solution, but crafting the right solution based on what you learn. Six months later, he referred two business owners to me. That's what happens when you adapt to solve problems instead of just maximizing rent checks.

THE MIT SCHOOL OF NEGOTIATION

The MIT School of Negotiation emphasizes data, logic, and analytical thinking to steer negotiations. They adopt a more systematic approach, ensuring decisions rely on facts and solid evidence rather than emotions or gut feelings. It's all about leveraging data and strategy to achieve the best possible outcome.

1. **Rely on Data-Driven Decision Making:** MIT's approach depends on collecting and analyzing data before and during negotiations. This may include market research, competitor analysis, or any other information that gives you an advantage. The goal is to support your arguments with substantial evidence.

2. **Maintain a Problem-Solving Mindset:** A negotiation is viewed as an effort to resolve a shared problem. Instead of seeing the other side as an opponent, you collaborate to find the best solution based on the facts.

3. **Use Systems Thinking:** The MIT approach looks at the bigger picture and how all the pieces connect. It's not just about what's happening now but also how this negotiation fits into a larger strategy or long-term plan.

4. **Optimize Outcomes:** MIT negotiators strive to find the most effective and valuable solution for both sides. They're not just after quick wins—they seek a deal that maximizes value for everyone.

In short, the MIT style focuses on using logic, data, and systems thinking to identify the best possible solution. It's a more analytical approach where emotions are less important than facts, aiming to optimize the outcome for everyone involved.

JIM'S PERSPECTIVE: I once coached a software CEO who was preparing to sell. He aimed for $225 million for his business. We explored every scenario and knew that it was a highly ambitious figure. When the best offer came in at $125 million, we didn't hesitate. We already had the logic in place. It wasn't what he wanted, but the data and prior transactions indicated it was a fair price, despite what the cocktail party consultants told him.

ONYI'S TAKE: Overthinking can kill a deal. Sometimes the upside is just obvious.

I've closed plenty of deals without diving deep into every scenario. Why? Because if a deal helps me hit my goal, the rest doesn't matter. You can spend weeks modeling every possible outcome, but most of those scenarios will never happen.

Focus on the scenarios that actually contribute to your end goal. Does this deal get me closer to where I want to be? Does it solve a real problem? Does it create the opportunity I'm looking for? If yes, and the downside is manageable, move forward.

Data has its place, but don't let analysis paralysis rob you of opportunities that are staring you in the face. Sometimes the best deals are the ones where you trust what you see instead of what the spreadsheet says.

NEVER SPLIT THE DIFFERENCE SCHOOL

Chris Voss, a former FBI hostage negotiator, wrote "Never Split the Difference" and offers a unique perspective on negotiations. He emphasizes emotional intelligence, psychological tactics, and tactical empathy. His approach involves reading people, understanding their emotions, and leveraging that insight to steer the conversation toward your desired outcome. It's like mental chess, where you're trying to get inside the other person's head.

1. **Develop Tactical Empathy:** Voss discusses "tactical empathy," which involves genuinely understanding

the other person's emotions and perspective. It's not just about being kind—it's about using that understanding to influence them effectively.

2. **Label Emotions:** One of his key tactics is to identify what the other person might be feeling. For example, saying, "It seems like you're frustrated with the current offer," can make the other person feel understood and more willing to negotiate.

3. **Leverage the Power of No:** Unlike most methods that aim for a "yes," Voss's approach encourages the other side to say "no." It gives them a sense of control and safety, which can help move the conversation forward.

4. **Tap into Mirroring:** Another technique is mirroring—in this case, repeating the last few words the other person said. It's a simple way to show you are listening and encourage the other person to explain more, giving you additional information to work with.

5. **Find the Black Swan:** Voss searches for hidden pieces of information—what he calls "black swans"—that can influence the negotiation. These are small details or motivations the other side isn't openly sharing, but if you uncover them, they can change the entire deal.

In summary, Chris Voss's negotiation approach focuses on psychology, emotions, and carefully guiding the other person through empathy and strategic communication. It emphasizes influencing the other party rather than relying solely on hard facts to reach a solution that benefits you.

JIM'S PERSPECTIVE: Useful when emotions are intense. It's especially helpful for high-stake, sensitive deals. Honestly, this is not my strongest mode of negotiation as I tend towards a logical approach as an engineer. However, when the other side has intense emotions on a topic, like leaving the name of the company the same after a sale—that can be used to gain advantage as they tend to overvalue that issue.

ONYI'S TAKE: I love this approach. Tactical empathy and demonstrating genuine commitment are incredibly powerful.

When I tell someone I'll invest my own money in a deal, it's not a pressure tactic, it's a signal of alignment. They see that I believe in it enough to put my own capital at risk. That shifts the conversation from "he's trying to sell me" to "we're evaluating this opportunity together."

And when you have a track record of success, they don't want to miss the opportunity to be part of it. This is what Voss calls removing the fear of loss. When people see you're willing to take the same risk you're asking them to take, they stop feeling like they're being sold and start feeling like they're being invited. That's not manipulation—that's earned credibility meeting partnership.

WINNER TAKES ALL SCHOOL

The "Winner Takes All" negotiation philosophy is exactly what it sounds like—it's all about grabbing as much as possible with little concern for the other side. This approach is aggressive and competitive, focused on winning at any cost. The goal is to dominate the negotiation and walk away with the best possible deal, even if the other party gets very little.

Negotiating with people who hold this philosophy is not fun; ideally, if you see it coming, you can walk away from the deal.

1. **Maximize Your Gain:** Your main goal is to get everything you want, regardless of what the other side asks. There's no emphasis on compromise or creating a win-win situation. It's all about your success.

2. **Play Hardball:** In this take-it-or-leave-it strategy, you use tough tactics like making extreme demands, refusing to back down, and applying pressure to force the other side to give in.

3. **Make Power Moves:** If you have the advantage, maximize that power. Use your strength—whether it's your position, resources, or information—to overpower the other side.

4. **Forget About Relationships:** Unlike more cooperative approaches, the winner-takes-all mindset doesn't prioritize building long-term relationships. The focus is solely on winning the deal, even if it means burning bridges.

5. **Focus on Short-Term Gains:** This approach often aims to secure the best deal quickly without considering long-term consequences. Once you've won, you move on to the next deal.

The "Winner Takes All" philosophy is about winning at all costs. It's aggressive and competitive, focused on maximizing your gains with little regard for the other side's needs or the long-term relationship. While this high-risk, high-reward approach can work in some situations, it might harm partnerships or hurt your reputation if used too often.

JIM'S PERSPECTIVE: This is the least sustainable strategy. It might win the deal, but you'll lose people and goodwill. I use it only if I know it's a one-time transaction with no recurring future payments or relationships. I used to work for a fellow that used this approach. I watched every deal he ever negotiated unwind after the handshake because the other side figured out he worked them over and created an unfair deal.

ONYI'S TAKE: With great power comes great responsibility. Not my quote, but a good one.

I've had plenty of deals where I held all the cards—where I could have taken everything and left the other side with scraps.

But here's what Winner-Takes-All negotiators miss: when someone loses in a deal, there's always a cost. Maybe they bad-mouth you to every person in the industry. Maybe they find ways to back out or underperform their obligations. Maybe they become a competitor who's now personally motivated to crush you. You might win the deal and lose everything else.

The negotiating table always has at least two sides. No one makes a deal unless there's something both parties want—and it's not always money. Sometimes it's reputation. Sometimes it's relationships. Sometimes it's the opportunity to do business again.

Winner-takes-all is extremely short-sighted. I'd rather structure a deal where the other side walks away thinking, "That was fair—I'd work with him again." Because the real win isn't maximizing this one deal. It's building a reputation where people want to bring you the next one.

LOSE-LOSE (YES, SERIOUSLY)

We have all been taught to seek a so-called "win-win" solution in negotiations, and many of these approaches promote that as well. But when you watch the best negotiators in action, you'll see they use a very different tactic. Their goal is to create what you might call "lose-lose" deals.

At first, "lose-lose" sounds like failure. But it's not. It means:

1. **Each party gives up what matters least.**
2. **Both get what they value most.**
3. **You uncover interests and create tailored trades.**

Consider the following example: Two people sat across from each other at a small wooden table, a single bright yellow lemon between them. Both needed it for an important project. The air was thick with tension as they discussed and debated, each making their case. After much back and forth, they finally arrived at what seemed like the fairest compromise—splitting the lemon in half. With a quick slice, the problem was "solved," and they each walked away with their share.

However, as they returned to their respective tasks, frustration began to set in. One person was crafting a batch of refreshing cocktails, but with only half a lemon, there wasn't nearly enough juice. The other was baking a delicate lemon cake, yet the small amount of zest they had wasn't sufficient to infuse the batter with the bright citrus flavor they had envisioned.

Only later did they realize—if they had asked each other why they needed the lemon, they could have both gotten exactly what they wanted. The cocktail maker could have taken all the juice, while the baker could have used all the zest.

This simple misunderstanding taught a valuable lesson: true negotiation isn't just about compromise; it's about discovering each other's real needs. When both sides take the time to listen and understand motivations, they can often find a solution that works for everyone.

The key is understanding what the other person in the deal is seeking. What do they need and why? The better you understand their issues and needs, the more likely you are to find a mutually beneficial solution. The goal is to see what the other party wants from the deal while also recognizing what you might not care about as much. These are ideal opportunities for painless compromise.

JIM'S PERSPECTIVE: It's not weakness. It's creative deal-making. If I give up something you want that I don't value,

I've lost nothing and gained everything. Finding the creative lose-lose can be a key element in a solution that both parties will honor.

ONYI'S TAKE: I once purchased a $4 million chain of salons from a bank after the owner ran into financial trouble. I paid off what he owed, securing favorable financing from the bank along with additional funds for new equipment and renovations. This allowed the bank to move a bad loan off its books and into its performing portfolio. I might have overpaid some but gained both equity and cash flow—a smart lose-lose.

In the next chapter, we'll cover what to do before the negotiation starts—how to prepare, gather intelligence, and develop your strategy.

But first, reflect: which style do you prefer, and which one might give you an advantage you haven't tapped into yet?

〉 CHAPTER ONE TAKEAWAYS 〈

1. **Context is everything.** Different negotiation styles (Harvard, Yale, Stanford, etc.) are effective in different situations— learn when to use each.

2. **Know your own tendencies.** Identifying your natural negotiation style helps you adapt to match the situation or counter your counterpart's approach.

3. **Creative compromise is strategic.** The best deals often come from understanding and trading what each party values most.

   Bonus—Pitfall to Avoid: Don't lead with the wrong style—or expect the other party to match yours.

BEFORE THE NEGOTIATION— WIN IT BEFORE YOU BEGIN

YOU WOULD BE SURPRISED at how many people enter a negotiation with no prior planning for their strategy. However, a successful negotiation starts long before the two parties step into the room. Strong negotiators don't just walk in blindly, hoping they'll achieve the highest price through gut feelings and intuition. Instead, they gather information that helps them anticipate their opponents' moves, identify leverage points and potential areas of compromise, and develop a strategy that ensures you get what you want from the negotiation.

Before sitting down at the negotiation table, you must gather as much information as possible about the deal. This isn't just about knowing what you want; it's also about understanding the other side. What are their goals? What pressure are they under? What can you offer them that's valuable?

That's because negotiation isn't just what happens at the table. The outcome is often decided before the first handshake. If you're not doing your homework, your opponent already has the advantage. Too many people treat negotiation like improv, but top negotiators prepare like chess players. They don't guess; they anticipate. What does that look like?

- They understand their own bottom line—and their ideal result.
- They analyze the other side's goals, needs, and constraints.
- They anticipate likely responses and prepare counters ahead of time.
- They know the going rate for what you're buying or selling. They know who else is bidding and what their BATNA (Best Alternative to a Negotiated Agreement) is.
- They anticipate objections. What might they push back on? Where will they question your terms? They prepare their answers.

The more context you have, the more confident you'll feel. The key to gathering valuable information for a negotiation is to look beyond the numbers and do thorough research on the other party. The more you learn about their business, goals, pain points, and track record, the better equipped you'll be to create a deal that gets you what you want on terms you agree to. Sometimes the best deal isn't the first one offered. That's why preparation isn't just about defense—it's about patience.

In this chapter, we'll teach you how to tilt the odds in your favor through strategy, psychology, and practical intelligence. Just remember: Preparation Isn't Optional.

Let's break down how to do it well.

KNOW YOUR WALKAWAY POINT

Decide what you want to achieve from the deal, or your "walk-away point," before entering any negotiation. This helps prevent you from agreeing to something that doesn't meet your needs.

Most negotiators start with their best-case scenario in mind, aiming for maximum value and minimum loss. However, the other step, which many overlook, is defining the most you're willing to give and the least you're willing to accept. For example, the CEO of a software company wants to sell his business. Ideally, he hopes to get $225 million for it. But what if the highest offer he receives is $125 million? Is that enough to close the deal?

Answering "How low will you go?" or "How high will you go?" is a very effective way to plan when you might need to leave a negotiation, unless some extraordinary terms come up. (More on balancing price versus terms later.) You need to know the point where the deal no longer makes sense for you, and it's time to walk away.

Your walkaway point is your anchor. Without it, you're

negotiating based on emotion. With it, you're operating from a strategy.

REAL LIFE NEGOTIATION—JIM: A company I worked for was consolidating the telecom test market through strategic acquisitions. There was one excellent California based company that we wanted and ultimately got into a bidding war, skillfully crafted by the sellers. We overpaid, badly. Worse, we used debt to finance the acquisition. When the market turned down (and telecom markets are cyclical), there wasn't enough cash flow to support the debt. That over payment nearly sunk the company.

REAL LIFE NEGOTIATION—ONYI: Before I enter any deal, I know my maximum and minimum. The person who cares less about the deal or is willing to walk away usually has the upper hand for a few reasons. If you're desperate for a deal, you'll likely be willing to make concessions. But if you're okay with walking away, you can hold firm on to your demands.

What's more, your readiness to walk away highlights your power and puts pressure on the other side to do what it takes to keep you at the table. So, before the negotiation begins, determine your "walk away" point. When you're at the table, don't bluff, but do be prepared to end the negotiation if the deal doesn't meet your minimum.

Once, I walked away from a $12 million acquisition because they asked for too much. I waited. The deal fell through with others. Months later, I bought it for less than I initially offered. If you're not willing to walk away, you're not negotiating.

KNOW WHAT THEY WANT—
EVEN IF THEY DON'T TELL YOU

We all carry hidden priorities to the table. The job of a negotiator is to uncover them. Ask questions. Listen between the lines. Sometimes, what they say they want isn't what they truly need. There are a couple of tools that can help you identify those needs.

"THE FIVE WHYS"

You may have some idea of the positions the other party will take in your negotiation, but as you're strategizing, resist the temptation to look at those positions as black-or-white. Knowing why they might be taking the stances they're taking can help you think creatively to strike a deal that solves both sides' problems (something we leaders love to do!).

When the other party in a negotiation presents goals that oppose yours, it can be helpful to understand the underlying issues driving those goals. However, extracting that information from the other team can be challenging. When this happens, and the figures don't add up for you, a technique called "The 5 Whys" can be very effective in gaining insight into the other side.

This tool helps you go beyond surface-level demands. Keep asking "why" until you discover their true motivation. Maybe they want a high price, but they need to show board approval. Or maybe they desire speed because of an expiring tax break. Dig deep. That's where the deal resides.

REAL LIFE NEGOTIATION—JIM: A word of caution: Some people might find this technique too intrusive or irritating. It can make some feel like they are being questioned, especially when you first start using it. Anyone with a 3-year-old will tell you this can get tedious.

But my experience shows that sticking with it can change people's behavior. They start to expect to be asked why, so they come prepared with answers. That becomes a win-win for the organization and your team because they begin to dig deeper into the root causes of problems before jumping to conclusions.

REACTION MATRIX

Once you know your bottom-line price and have considered your opponent's needs and motivations, it's time to develop your game plan. You can organize this plan as a "Reaction Matrix." Just as a grandmaster can visualize the first ten moves of a chess game in their mind, you can create a spreadsheet to outline the moves—and countermoves—you might encounter in your negotiation.

While some people might consider how someone could

react to their initial proposal—if I do this, then they'll likely do that—the real magic happens when you take it to the next level. And even further, the level beyond that. Think through the likely back-and-forth. What will they say when you counter? What will you say when they push back? Build a script three moves deep.

In other words, you've thought ahead and mapped out your moves based on your opponent's reactions three layers deep. That is a three-level reaction matrix, and it can be a powerful advantage.

REAL LIFE NEGOTIATION—JIM: I have used this method during a negotiation and nearly laughed out loud when everything unfolded exactly as I had anticipated. You might not think this is possible, but most negotiation moves are predictable as are the responses. The issue is most people won't drive the logic three levels deep. I had spent many sleepless nights beforehand considering parameters, moves, and countermoves, so the game day was predictable. The lack of sleep was well worth the result. We practice hard so the games are easy.

LEVERAGE: FIND IT OR CREATE IT

In any negotiation, it's not just about what you want. It's about what the other side wants, too. The more you know about their goals and challenges, the more leverage you'll have.

So, during your negotiation preparations, spend some time thinking like your opponent. Try to understand their perspective to grasp better what they want from the talks. This is especially important if their goals differ from yours. If you can figure out the other side's motivation, you can better predict their moves.

For example, if you're selling your rapidly growing company to a larger corporation, your needs and the buyer's might differ significantly. As the founder, you aim to sell the company, protect your team, and position it for continued success. In contrast, leadership on the buyer's side is more focused on minimizing risk and making sure the deal doesn't backfire, which could harm their career. This understanding means they might prioritize price over risk, creating a key opportunity in the negotiation.

If you think like the buyer and discover what matters most to them, you can better understand how to negotiate and structure the deal to protect against downside and risk levels while maximizing your price. What's most powerful is when this prep work allows you to give concessions to your opponent that they value—but that mean far less to you. The better you understand your opponent, the more you can predict their behavior and offer them terms you know will get the deal done. Terms you are happy to provide.

Understanding your leverage in a negotiation is like knowing the strength of a poker hand. It's what gives you power in the game. Your leverage includes what you bring to the table that makes you unique, what the other side needs from you, and what alternatives you have if this deal falls through.

Knowing your leverage helps you set realistic goals and make confident decisions based on the power you bring to the negotiation. It also helps you avoid being taken advantage of if the other side tries to exploit you. You can also address objections before they happen to maintain control. "You might be wondering why our price is higher. Let me show you why it's worth it."

Leverage isn't just what you have—it's what they think you have.

REAL LIFE NEGOTIATION—ONYI: Understanding your leverage in a negotiation is understanding what you bring to the table that the other side actually needs. Your leverage consists of what makes you unique, what the other side needs from you, and what alternatives you have if this deal falls through.

Knowing your leverage helps you set realistic goals and make informed decisions. It also helps you avoid being taken advantage of if the other side tries to exploit you.

Here's the thing about leverage: sometimes you have more than you think, even when it looks like you have nothing.

When I was 21 years old, a college student with no money, I wanted to buy a supplement store. The owner wanted $99,000 for it. On paper, I had zero leverage: no money, no business experience, no track record. She had all the cards— she owned the business, and I was broke.

But I dug deeper to understand the real situation. She wanted to sell because the business was losing money or breaking even—basically a waste of her time. That was my leverage. She needed a buyer who could actually turn it around, not just someone with cash.

So I positioned myself differently. I was a local bodybuilder with influence in the fitness industry. I knew that community, understood the products, and could drive traffic she couldn't. I wasn't just asking to buy her business, I was offering to save it.

We made a deal: she owner-financed the entire $99K on a 5-year note at 5% interest. I paid it off in 18 months and increased sales by over 250%.

That's what understanding leverage really means—finding what you bring to the table that the other side actually needs, even when it's not obvious.

PRACTICE THE ART OF PERSUASION

At its core, a negotiation is all about convincing someone to change their mind—to give you what you want. The challenge is figuring out how to do that. Once you have your strategy in place, you need to think about how to carry it out—meaning, how to communicate with the opposing party to effectively bring your plan to life. You can consider persuading someone to see things your way in two different ways.

The first way to persuade is to use logic and reason. Think about how you'd approach buying a car. The first step might be to look at all the data to help you decide: what kind of gas mileage does it get, what are its reliability ratings, what is the size of its trunk, and so on. By analyzing all this data, you can make a very logical decision about the best car to buy.

While you might think someone could be persuaded just with the facts, you could miss out on opportunity by not tapping into the second persuasion pathway: emotions. After all, we know there's another way we might be persuaded to buy that car. That path is rooted in emotions and intuition. In this case, we might be influenced by whether we know someone else who owns a similar vehicle, maybe even a big-name celebrity. We might also be persuaded by how the car's color makes you feel or even if you smile a lot while test-driving it. Here, you're less concerned with data and more focused on your feelings.

Of course, the marketing and sales teams at the dealership know that you rely on both logic and emotion to make these decisions, and they tap into both by offering all the details and numbers you could want, along with imagery and stories that sell the experience of driving this car, showing you how purchasing it can "make you the kind of person you want to be."

As you prepare for your negotiation, consider these two approaches. What are the logical bases for your arguments, and what emotional appeals can you use to make the other party feel personally connected to your position?

When you have both logic and emotions available, how

do you decide which levers to pull? As the great Zig Ziglar said, "If you only use facts to make a sale, you will have the best-educated prospect in the world. But when you can also use emotion, that's when you have a customer." In other words, the best strategy might be to engage prospects emotionally and provide just enough facts based on the risk level of the decision to help them decide. How to balance the two often depends on the stakes involved in the negotiation—whether it's something that could sink your boat or not. For low-risk situations, pulling the emotional lever might lead to great business results. However, the higher the stakes, the more your approach should be logical and rational, while still providing emotional context.

In short, when preparing your negotiation strategies, remember there are two main ways to persuade people. Sometimes, you should focus on the facts, while other times, you need to appeal to someone's emotions. Both methods can be powerful, so don't miss the chance to use them to your advantage.

REAL LIFE NEGOTIATION—ONYI: FOMO (Fear of Missing Out) is one of the most powerful forces in negotiation—and the key is making sure YOU'RE not the one feeling it.

Avoiding FOMO: Stay in Your Buy Box   I always stay within my buy box. That means I have clear formulas for what I'm willing to pay. For a commercial building, if I can't increase the value by a minimum of 50%, and ideally 100%, through my improvements, I don't touch it. Period.

It doesn't matter how much I love the building, where it's located, or how badly I think I need it. I never let FOMO push me into a bad deal. I stay patient, and I've never not been rewarded for that patience. Everything always works out.

Using Others' FOMO to Your Advantage   A few years ago, I had a deal lined up to buy three salon locations in Dallas from the same owner. We had an APA written up, financials reviewed, everything ready to close. At the twenty-third hour, the seller tried to renegotiate and push for more money. I refused and walked away.

He went to one of our competitors and told them: "Onyi's going to buy this if you don't." They had FOMO. They over-paid—$2.5 million for all three locations.

Here's what happened next: We only wanted two of those three stores anyway. The third was too close to our Addison location, and we wanted it closed. The competitor closed it themselves. Our nearby store is up 60% since they closed it— and we got that for free.

Then we just opened brand new locations in the other two markets—new equipment, nicer buildouts, no baggage from existing customers. Same net result, zero dollars spent on acquisition, better long-term position.

The lesson? When you're patient and disciplined, other people's FOMO works in your favor. They chase deals emotionally. You build strategically. And you win.

USE QUESTIONS AS WEAPONS

Another key skill to develop when preparing for a negotiation is asking questions. Observing successful CEOs, you notice they don't rely on their titles to influence others. Instead, top CEOs use open-ended questions to help people generate solutions they naturally support. These conversations can be skillfully guided toward answers that the CEO can agree with, even if those answers aren't exactly what they would have chosen.

Let's say you want to change the compensation program within your organization. One way to try implementing that change is by issuing an order: "We are going to change the comp plan," you might say. However, do you think your team will be motivated to carry out that plan? Probably not, in my opinion. You might even face significant resistance from within the organization because people don't understand why you want to make the change in the first place. The usual first response to sudden change is to hit the brakes.

But what if you started the process by asking open-ended questions instead? Maybe you could begin by asking questions like: What is the cost of keeping our compensation plan the way it is? What would happen if we changed our compensation plan? What could we accomplish if we changed our compensation plan?

Asking open-ended questions like these encourages people to give longer answers instead of just Yes or No.

The strength of this approach is that it secures buy-in from the people answering the questions. Instead of being told what to do, they create the plan themselves—which gives them a much stronger sense of ownership and involvement in making it happen.

The same principle holds true in negotiations. You likely won't have much success convincing the other party by saying, "This is how I want it." The more you try to tell anyone what to think, the more resistant they will become. The skill lies in asking carefully thought-out, open-ended questions to prevent someone from viewing "your" point of view as if it's their own. If you do that, you're much more likely to reach mutually agreeable terms. When people articulate their logic, they're more likely to accept your solution.

Think about preparing questions ahead of time like:

- What would success look like for you here?
- What are your biggest concerns?
- Why is that important to you?

FIND COMMON GROUND

We have all experienced disagreements with others, whether in business or personal life. No matter the situation, arguing can be emotionally draining when you can't understand why the other person doesn't see things the same way. However, you can turn any argument into a productive discussion by helping both sides find common ground.

To do this, we can learn from Peter Senge's classic book, *The Fifth Discipline*. It's a dense book filled with many helpful tips and techniques, but I want to focus on his "Ladder of Inference." In short, Senge's ladder has four parts:

1. Data
2. Personal Experience Filter
3. Processing
4. Conclusions

We all start with some form of data, which we use to work toward forming an opinion or conclusion. We then apply our filters—past experiences and biases that add color or subjective value to that information. Finally, we use whatever educational or professional training we may have gained over time to process that filtered information into what we believe is a well-formed conclusion.

The main issue most of us face when we argue is that we're debating our conclusions at the top of the Ladder of Inference. However, we might not be comparing apples to apples because we may not have used the same data, filters, or processing methods to reach those conclusions.

If we want to find common ground, we need to be willing to disclose our Ladders of Inference to each other. That means sharing where you each got your data from to be sure you're starting from the same foundation.

Then, it's time to talk about your filters and how you interpret that data. This is where personal experience can strongly influence your perspective. For instance, if you once played poker and someone wearing a red hat cheated, you might develop a bias, believing that everyone with a red hat cheats at poker. That might sound unlikely, but it shows how our minds work—and it can be a key factor in shaping an argument.

More seriously, if you have a PhD in statistics and are an expert in probability, you might have a different opinion than someone else about your odds of success in that poker game or what you should bet if you draw a pair of aces.

Often, a whole argument can be resolved—or a deal made in a negotiation—by understanding the data each party is using and how they interpret it. Neither of us is technically "wrong," which opens a path to finding common ground. Of course, you might not agree, but you will understand precisely why you disagree without the emotion, and you can use this newfound common ground to reach a resolution that works for everyone.

As you prepare for your negotiation, outline your own ladders of inference so you can share them with the other party when needed—and write down some questions that will help you explore their ladders to find common ground.

FROM GAME PLAN TO GAME TIME

A well-run negotiation is never won at the table—it's won in the preparation leading up to it. That's what separates great negotiators from everyone else. They don't just show up with confidence. They show up with clarity, data, and a strategy built three steps deep. They know where they'll walk away, where they'll bend, and how to speak to both the logic and emotion of the other party.

Here's the bottom line: If you fail to prepare, you're preparing to lose. Whether it's defining your walkaway point, uncovering the other side's hidden motivations, crafting a reaction matrix, or sharpening your leverage, preparation is where deals are made or broken.

Let's recap:

- **Preparation wins more deals than charisma ever will.** Negotiators who do their homework have options—and options give you power.
- **Know what matters to you—and what matters to them.** Understanding both sides of the table unlocks creative paths to yes.
- **Plan three moves deep.** Don't just imagine your opening line—build a playbook for their likely response, and your counter to it.

And one last reminder:

- **Don't improvise.** The best way to lose a negotiation is to make it up as you go. That's how you end up chasing their agenda instead of advancing your own.

Now that you've developed your game plan, it's time to engage in the negotiation. In the next chapter, we'll introduce you to tactics that bring your preparation to life—how to make your initial ask, how to handle pressure, and how to stay steady in the heat of the moment.

Get ready to enter the ring.

⟩ CHAPTER TWO TAKEAWAYS ⟨

1. **Preparation beats improvisation.** The majority of a negotiation's success is determined before it starts—through research, goal-setting, and strategic planning.

2. **Know your walkaway point.** Defining your non-negotiables in advance gives you power and prevents emotional decision-making.

3. **Understand their needs—even the hidden ones.** Asking the right questions (e.g., using "The Five Whys") uncovers the other party's real motivations.

TACTICS FOR A SUCCESSFUL NEGOTIATION

ONCE YOU UNDERSTAND THE mindset of a strong negotiator, the next step is to build your toolkit—the practical tactics that help you turn confidence and strategy into real results. Negotiation isn't just about what you want; it's about how you pursue it. What you say, how you respond, when you pause, and even when you crack a joke—all of these things matter.

In this chapter, we'll break down some of the most effective techniques we've used and taught over the years. You'll learn how to build rapport with "Tell, Ask, Connect, Sell," how to use silence as a weapon, how anchoring sets expectations, and when to walk away. These aren't abstract theories. They're practical tools you can apply in a deal—whether you're buying a building, negotiating a salary, or closing a company acquisition.

Think of this chapter as your negotiation guide—the strategies that help you gain leverage, build trust, and direct the conversation in your favor. Let's begin with two proven strategies to kick off the negotiation effectively.

TELL, ASK, CONNECT, SELL

When trying to do business with someone and ultimately want him or her to make a purchase or agree during a complex negotiation, there is a little secret you can use to significantly improve your success rate. It all comes down to following a simple sequence: tell, ask, connect, and sell.

1. TELL

Your first goal is to introduce yourself to potential customers. Although that may seem easy, it can sometimes be overlooked in today's digital age. Your goal should be to share some personal details about yourself in a natural, conversational manner that helps others connect with you on a deeper level. You might talk about your alma mater, favorite book, or movie. Be authentic and choose something you genuinely care about. Using a self-deprecating sense of humor can work well in this context.

2. ASK

Your second step is to ask them questions about their lives or interests. You can use a method described in Barbara Walters's book, *How to Talk to Anybody About Anything*. It shows how to ask someone questions in five different categories.

- Ask them about their family or children.
- Ask them about a book they have read recently.
- Ask about their hobbies.
- Ask about any trip they have made recently.
- Ask them about their vacation plans.

One caveat is that this approach works best in the U.S. since other international cultures tend to be less willing to share personal information. The truth is, you need to genuinely care about asking these questions and listening to the answers you receive. Don't ask and then go back to Candy Crush on your phone, because that relates to the next step...

3. CONNECT

Find a connection with your potential customer or partner based on something you both share. You'll be amazed at how quickly you can find these common threads, ranging from having kids of the same age, people you both know, attending the same school, or having a shared interest in a particular area of the world to visit.

Making these connections is vital to building trust and a bond with people, without which they will be much less interested in becoming your customers or partners.

REAL LIFE NEGOTIATION—JIM: The first portion of any connection is to establish connection. There are plenty of ways to find connection, when you grew up, mutual friends, mutual interests or travel, One example was a conversation with a potential client in Connecticut, where I used to live. I helped run a PGA Tour golf tournament for many years there, and once I disclosed this, it turned out his firm had sponsored the tournament for years. It was an instant connection and made the negotiation smooth and easy.

4. SELL

If you can develop connections with people by first sharing and then asking through genuine conversation and active listening to find connections, you will increase your chances of successfully selling something by an order of magnitude. That's because people don't like to buy from anyone they don't know or trust.

We all know the person who jumps ahead in this sequence and goes straight to their sales pitch without taking the time to establish a connection.

Sure, we might be willing to buy something transactionally from someone we don't know on the street or online. But if you're trying to develop the relationships that lead to years of repeat business and lifetime customers, following this secret will pay off big time.

FLINCH, REFLECT, GO SILENT

Through our experiences receiving offers from opposing parties, we have both come to rely on a simple three-step process
that delivers almost every time: flinch, reflect, and remain
silent.

1. FLINCH

When someone quotes a price, it's probably human nature to
avoid embarrassment and respond by saying, "That's reasonable." But if your goal is to negotiate that price down, that's
the worst possible response. Instead, when someone shares
a price with you, you're better off displaying some "flinch"—
perhaps reacting as if the person slapped you. Jim's preference
is a verbal response like "oomph" or sucking air through my
teeth to indicate my physical displeasure at hearing that price
quoted. The point is to communicate your discontent with the
price in a clear quick manner—no matter how reasonable the
price really is. This is a time to remember your drama class
and go big on the flinch.

2. REFLECT

After showing your physical displeasure with the initial quote,
your next move is to repeat to that person what they said in a
way that reinforces how steep you think it is. Let's say you're

trying to buy a rug at a flea market, and the vendor quotes you a price of $100. After flinching, you might say something like: "$100 for this rug?" or simply "$100?" The point is to communicate how shocked and displeased you are by the price they are quoting you.

3. GO SILENT

The last step in negotiating a better price is to go silent. Be warned: this is highly uncomfortable for you and the other party. But it's also extremely effective because, at some point, someone will be moved to break the silence. Remember the rule: whoever speaks first loses. Your goal is to keep your mouth closed, even if every second seems to drag on for minutes at a time. Just staying quiet for 20 seconds can seem like an hour. But remember, don't speak up. One tip Jim uses is to bite his tongue (softly) to ensure that he doesn't break the silence. The prior two steps set up this decisive final move in gaining a concession.

If you can master these three steps—flinch, reflect, and go silent—you'll discover that you can secure significant concessions from the person you're negotiating with, whether you're bargaining over a yard sale coffee mug or involved in a high-stakes deal to buy a company. We recommend trying it in a smaller setting first to learn the technique so you can become comfortable with it.

REAL LIFE NEGOTIATION—ONYI: I negotiate every deal for my franchisees, from leases to competitor buyouts. After the franchisee and I discuss our maximum and desired prices, I tell them not to react, even if the seller's offer falls within our range.

Why? Because price is only one piece of the puzzle.

Even if the number looks good, we need time to analyze the full terms. What are the lease escalations? What's included in the buildout allowance? What are the operating expense caps? The details matter, and knee-jerk decisions lead to missed red flags.

I've seen buyers respond to offers with an immediate "Yes, we can do that," only to realize later they agreed to terms that don't actually work. Or worse, the seller interprets that quick yes as a signal they could have asked for more—and they come back trying to renegotiate.

The Value of Reflection Even if the price is exactly what we want, we don't react except to say, "Okay, let us discuss this and see if we can make it work." Then we take time to review everything properly.

This does two things: First, it ensures we actually analyze the full deal, not just the headline number. Second, it signals that we're serious, thoughtful buyers who do our homework. When we come back and accept, the seller knows we've vetted the deal thoroughly, which actually builds confidence on both sides.

When the Number Isn't Right If the number isn't what we wanted, we flinch, reflect, and go quiet. But this isn't about playing games—it's about giving ourselves space to think and giving them space to reconsider.

Here's what often happens: When you don't immediately reject or counteroffer, the other person has time to sit with their own number. Sometimes they'll start talking through their thinking out loud: "Well, I think we can figure something out, but that is what I wanted."

That's not anxiety—that's them processing. And when people process out loud, they often talk themselves into flexibility. They're signaling they want to make the deal work, and they're opening the door to negotiation without you having to push.

The lesson? Take time to think. Negotiation isn't just about what you say—it's about giving yourself time to make good decisions. When you stay composed and thoughtful, even when an offer seems attractive, you catch details others miss. Don't rush. Don't react. Analyze, then respond.

NEGOTIATING PRO TIPS

With these two ready-made strategies in mind, let's consider some best practices that will help you keep the negotiation smooth, transparent, and on course for an agreeable resolution.

1. CONSIDER TERMS AS WELL AS PRICE

One of the most common things Jim has noticed when a founder or CEO sells their company is that they become enamored with the price they get for the business. The headline they focus on the most is, "I sold it for $XX million!" We even see this in professional sports, where free agents can become obsessed with signing a record contract with the highest total value, even when it means leaving a team that offered more per year.

While there's nothing wrong with earning the most money you can from selling your business (or spending as little as you can if you're in the buyer's seat), if you get stuck on price, you might overlook a critical component of any deal: the terms.

Let's say we want to buy your business from you, and your asking price is $50 million. Now, let's also say that we agree with your asking price, with a catch: we want to dictate the terms of the deal. Why? Because, in many ways, we might end up paying far less than $50 million for your business.

One example might be inserting a term in the contract that states we will place 20 percent of the $50 million selling price ($10 million) in escrow for five years, and it will only be paid out if certain conditions are met. Depending on those conditions, there is a genuine chance you just sold me your business for $40 million.

Another example would be a contract term where we

will pay you $30 million at the time of the sale, but you need to "earn out" the other $20 million based on the company hitting specific financial targets. While those targets might seem reasonable at first, you must remember that you no longer control the business as you once did, which could make reaching those targets challenging. In that case, you just sold your company for $30 million. We hope you didn't buy a yacht with the extra $20 you'll never see.

The point is that there are many ways each side of the negotiation can structure the terms of a deal, which could also include warranties and representations, to influence the actual dollar value significantly. That's why, if we have a choice between controlling the price of the deal or the terms, I'll choose the terms every time—even if it means trading some dollars for a smoother transaction and more favorable terms. In other words, your focus should always be on your price, not my terms.

REAL LIFE NEGOTIATION—JIM: Here's a pro tip for you: there's a reason savvy buyers and sellers have their attorneys draft the purchase or sale agreement. It allows them to control the terms. I've seen owners flinch at the $25,000 fee a lawyer charges, quickly accepting the other party's offer to have their attorney draft the agreement. They're happy to avoid the cost and hassle, but they might not realize they could be losing a lot of money in the long run. In any serious negotiation, look beyond the price and aim to own the deal's terms. That's how you'll win in the long run.

REAL LIFE NEGOTIATION—ONYI: I sold most of my tanning business at one point for the first time. I was 30 years old when my largest competitor approached me and said they wanted to buy. I had no interest in selling at that time. I was single with no kids, doing well for myself. I was making good money and had very little responsibility. Still, I agreed to a meeting, and they made me an offer that—price wise—I couldn't refuse. All my debt would be paid, and I'd walk away with seven figures after closing.

I was so excited that I didn't pay attention to the terms. The total price mattered to me, and a short closing window was crucial because I was going to Europe in two weeks. I didn't pay much attention to the fact that the terms meant I wouldn't receive the 2nd half final payment—in the seven figures—until a year later.

I would never agree to that deal knowing what I know now, but at the time I was just excited to have more money go into my account than I had ever had before. What I realized later was that they used the income from my stores to pay me that remaining seven-figure amount—because my stores produced a good portion of that each year. Essentially, I financed their payment for them at 0% interest, losing out on a lot of potential upsides. I was young and overexcited, and I learned a lot about negotiations. The buyer had figured out what I wanted, which was a quick close and high number, and then they established terms that were favorable to them.

2. ACT IN GOOD FAITH, FROM BEGINNING TO END

One of Jim's favorite definitions of "ethics" is what you do when no one else is watching, including the hidden cameras. In other words, how do you act when you're faced with different situations at work?

Hollywood has helped spread the stereotype that businesspeople lack ethics. The common belief is that succeeding in business requires doing whatever it takes, even if it means breaking laws or regulations. From his personal experience, Jim has seen that the opposite is often true. Although those who operate outside ethical boundaries might see some short-term benefits, they usually fall behind in the long run, especially when aiming to build a sustainable business or a long-term career.

Later in his career, shortly after he joined a new company as CEO, Jim received a package in the mail from an anonymous sender. Inside was a folder of secret material from our arch-competitor, including customer names, a sales funnel with bids, and price lists. This was a gold mine of competitive data that we could have used to give us an incredible edge in the market. So, what did he do? He bundled everything up and mailed it to the CEO of Jim's competitor. Jim then called him to let him know what Jim had done while also letting him know that he likely had a problem employee somewhere who had sent that information over. And that was the end of it.

Or at least Jim thought it was. Five years later, he ran into that CEO at a trade show. It was the first time they had ever met in person. When they shook hands, the CEO turned to his associate and said about Jim: "This is one of the ethical guys in the industry." He clearly remembered me and what I had done and found it remarkable. Jim supposes it was depressing that he didn't consider it completely normal.

Interestingly, Jim later bought that business—which might never have happened if he hadn't done the right thing years earlier.

So, while Hollywood may suggest that businesspeople succeed by cutting corners and acting unethically, the opposite is true. Anyone aiming to build a long-lasting and profitable business career understands that establishing long-term relationships based on trust is key, not by cheating anyone for short-term gains. Therefore, no matter how intense the negotiation or how high the stakes, it is crucial to keep your own behavior above reproach. This might mean accepting smaller short-term wins, but it will likely lead to greater success in the long run. More importantly, it allows you to look yourself in the mirror every day without guilt.

NEGOTIATION INSIGHTS—ONYI: One of my core values in business is ensuring that no one can legitimately say that I have screwed them over, no matter what.

I ensure that all my franchisees maximize their profits by helping them save as much money as possible. This increases their profitability, allowing them to open more stores. The more stores they open, the more franchise fees we collect, and the more money we make.

During the first five years of franchising, I didn't make a single dollar. I lost money not because revenue wasn't coming in, but because I was focused on making sure the franchisees were as profitable as possible and our operations were as strong as they could be. I invested every dollar we earned back into R&D, technology, and consultants to improve us. This effort made our FDD one of the best anyone had ever experienced, with no unhappy franchisees, and we've never had a store close. This approach allowed us to grow in the right way.

I realized I made more money when I stopped focusing on short-term financial gain. That is what we mean by playing the long game.

3. START FROM A REALISTIC POSITION

It's always wise to start (or anchor) with a slightly higher offer or demand than what you expect to receive. This gives you room to negotiate and helps the other side feel like they're getting a good deal. Just be careful not to go so far that you seem unreasonable. Negotiation can become very intense as both sides try to influence the outcome. Successful negotiations rely on trust and respect. Starting from an unrealistic position can quickly ruin a deal. This isn't just a math problem; it's about maintaining your credibility and possibly your relationship with the other party by avoiding wildly inappropriate offers.

For example, let's say we have identified a company we'd like to buy, and we know it's worth $5 million. But when we approach the business owner about selling for that price, he shakes his head and says his company is worth $20 million based on what someone told him at a cocktail party. While there might be a range of reasonable values around $5 million, his request for $20 million isn't close. It's unreasonable.

That puts us in a tough spot. We're unsure if this guy is truly serious about selling his business. We know what his company's worth, and when he asks for such an unrealistic price, I don't have much hope that we can reach an agreement—or that he respects me as a fellow businessperson.

In this situation, we would probably walk away. Even if he were to come back to me in a few years, genuinely interested in selling this time and with a more reasonable number in mind, we would hesitate. Putting us (and possibly others) off with that absurd number has damaged his reputation and credibility, which could hurt future offers.

The good news is that there are better ways to manage the beginning of a negotiation without overbidding or underbidding yourself out of the game.

One approach is to present a range of prices, understanding

that the terms can allow a deal even if you don't exactly reach your target number. Returning to our example of the company I wanted to buy, I might offer the seller a range of $5 million to $10 million, with different terms linked to each price point.

The seller might still prefer to ask for more money, but I could request better terms, like paying over an extended period. Either way, this approach has allowed us to start a conversation we might not have had if I had tried to lowball the offer, hoping we'd meet somewhere in the middle.

We advise you to be cautious of any advice that urges you to bid very low or ask for very high prices during negotiations. Stay alert to the real risks involved in doing this. Not only could you jeopardize the deal right from the start, but you might also damage your reputation and credibility, which could follow you in future negotiations.

REAL LIFE NEGOTIATION—ONYI: In business negotiations, if you name a price first, you lose control. You give up your power, limit your options, and risk either offering too little (and seeming not to be a serious contender) or paying much more than your target is worth.

Instead of immediately throwing out a number, try asking questions, emphasizing value, and using open-ended statements that foster mutual benefit. Allowing the other side to make the first move helps you gather information and maintain control of the negotiation.

4. USE ANCHORING TO SET EXPECTATIONS

Anchoring is a method to set expectations early in a negotiation, making your actual offer more appealing to the other party.

For example, let's say we're trying to sell a car and would love to get $25,000. We aim to anchor at a price point higher than my target sales price. We might say to a prospective buyer, "I've done a lot of research, and cars like mine typically sell for over $30,000. We recently saw one sell for $35,000."But then we'll add, "But it's got high mileage and will need some maintenance soon, so we're willing to take a bit less."

See what we did there? We've set a price point in the buyer's mind without letting them know we would be willing to take $25,000 for the car. Subsequent negotiations will occur from the anchor point, and I am happy to make concessions since we anchored high.

The same principle applies to the buyer. If we're interested in buying that car, we might start the negotiation by saying something like, "We just saw two cars like yours sell for $20,000." Then, we'll follow up by saying, "But we know they're rare, so we're willing to pay a bit more than the market rate to get one for ourselves."

Again, I've set the anchor at $20,000, but we are willing to negotiate from there to help close the deal with the seller.

Anchoring can also be used effectively in complex

negotiations like selling companies. A good example is when you need to negotiate the escrow amount in a deal. Escrow is a percentage of the purchase price held back in case something goes wrong. The seller wants that percentage to be as low as possible, while the buyer wants the opposite to help cover potential risks.

REAL LIFE NEGOTIATION—JIM: Once, when I was selling a company, a buyer told us they had researched recent transactions and said the average escrow was 8 percent of the purchase price. However, they were willing to lower it to 6.5 percent of the transaction value.

This move caught me off guard— it was a strong use of anchoring. They had data! No matter how much I tried to dispute their number, settling on the 6.5 percent made sense.

This technique can easily be applied in salary negotiations, especially if you adopt a strategy from my buyer's approach and bring data. One of the worst (and potentially illegal) questions anyone can face in an interview is, "How much do you want to make?" It always puts the interviewee in a difficult position. To counter that, bring data to the table that you can use to anchor the negotiation.

You might say, "I have researched this position, and jobs like the one you offer pay as high as $125,000." You're referencing $125,000 but willing to accept the position for $100,000. Again, you've created some wiggle room to help move the negotiation in your favor.

A word of caution: Watch for false anchors and weasel words, red flags that suggest the other side may be fudging their data. Phrases like, "as high as" or "as low as" are good indicators that something is off. And it's important to double check the data the other side presents. After all, as one of my favorite quotes says: "82% of all statistics are made up."

REAL LIFE NEGOTIATION—ONYI: At one time, I had my eye on a standalone building in East Texas. It was listed on CoStar along with another building next door, but I only wanted the single standalone property, which would be perfect for a Glo Tanning location.

I offered $1.15 million for the single building, but the agent said they had an offer for $1.35 million and turned it down. However, I knew that the group of partners selling the building wanted to ensure that, if they got just the single building under contract, the buyer would be able to close. I discussed my track record and strategy of purchasing real estate for Glo Tanning with my agent, my wife, and the managing partner. At that point, we were a national company with locations in 21 states. That impressed the seller, and we settled at $1.15 million.

During this deal, the appraiser messed up by providing three values for the building: one for $880,000 based on the current under-market lease, another with the building empty for 1.1 million and another for $1.85 million based on my plans to remodel the building and have Glo Tanning in it.

Using the empty value, I was able to go back and renegotiate the price down by $50,000, but I had to make the earnest money go hard and end the due diligence period. We now closed in 30 days.

The day before closing, my banker realized that the loan approval was based on the AS- IS value. They would finance 80% of the $880,000, not the new $1.1 million price. That increased my out-of-pocket cost by $220,000. I wanted to extend the closing to get bank approval to finance at the higher value, but that would take time we didn't have. The seller didn't want to extend—they were probably already counting the money. However, I was able to extend the closing by locking up an additional $75,000 in earnest money to extend the closing by 30 days so I could figure it out. This provided some assurances, and since that money was going toward my down payment, it kept my out-of-pocket expenses lower where I needed them to be.

5. BE WILLING TO WALK AWAY

Although we'll provide you with many strategies to handle difficult negotiators, there will be times when, during a negotiation, the other party might keep pushing and pushing to the point where the deal becomes unbalanced from your perspective. When this happens, you need to have the confidence to walk away, knowing you did your best. This is one of the strongest positions you can take in a negotiation because it shows confidence and can often pressure the other side to make concessions. Just make sure that walking away is a real option, not a bluff.

REAL LIFE NEGOTIATION—ONYI: The best deals I have made are the ones I didn't go through with. You need to know when to walk away because many of those deals come back around with better terms. I once had a real estate deal for a plaza where we signed a lease and had a first right of refusal on the building. We saw the deal when it hit the market. They wanted $5,450,000 for the building, which was a fair price. However, it needed a lot of remodeling, and the tenants weren't the best. I tried to negotiate the price down to $5 million, but they refused and had another offer from a group out of California. I advised them to take that offer, and they did, going under contract. I stayed in contact with the realtor, checking in biweekly. Finally, the realtor called me and said he thought the deal might come back and be available again.

I was able to gather some background on the owner and understand what they needed to ensure they had a win. Their major concern was to make sure it would close. So, I told them, "Listen, I will get approval from the bank first and completely underwrite the deal before going under contract. When we do go under contract, I will give $50k in earnest money, which goes hard on day 1. If I try to cancel the deal, I would lose $50k." The realtor had a letter from my bank confirming the deal was approved for financing, and I put up $50k.

What did I want in exchange? I aimed to lower the price to $5 million, but I already had approval for the larger amount. So, I requested it be written as the full asking price with a $500,000 seller credit, which effectively reduced my down payment by that amount. I also wanted the 2% buyer realtor commission credited toward my down payment, and I asked the seller to hold a $500k second note at 2 points below prime. They agreed to all my demands because I was able to meet their needs first. I was able to close on a $5.5 million property with only 6% down.

I knew that the rents were currently 50% below market because the center needed remodeling, and the old owner refused to invest in the building or re-tenant the spaces; he wanted the least resistance. The building has been remodeled with a more modern façade and is now in the process of re-tenanting the spaces. Once completed, the building's value will exceed $13 million, and the actual purchase price was $4.9 million with only 6% down.

6. USE SILENCE

In her book, *Quiet*, Susan Cain argues that sometimes remaining silent can be much more powerful than speaking. In other words, there is real power in silence. This message offers some lessons on how we handle conversations and negotiations.

Consider the example of someone asking you a question, then beginning to speak again immediately to fill the void of silence. They were never really interested in your answer anyway, and they will never learn anything from or about you, which can become a significant liability in a negotiation. The more you speak, the less information you will get in return.

What happens when a salesperson doesn't know how to be silent? They have to intuit how the other person feels about the deal. That's why a better technique is asking a question and then biting your lip. Say nothing—even as ten or 15 seconds of awkward silence pass. While you might not realize it, you are gaining power by staying quiet instead of filling the space with noise and energy.

As a side note, this is why one of the most underrated tactics in negotiation is listening. Too often, people come into negotiations so focused on their goals that they forget to pay attention to what the other side is saying. But listening is where you find out what the other side wants and where opportunities for compromise or creativity lie. This means not just hearing the words but understanding the feelings and concerns behind them. It also means recognizing that what isn't said is just as important as what is. Pay attention to body language, tone of voice, and what the other side might avoid. These can give you clues about their true priorities.

Another advantage of staying silent is that you can often sit back and watch the other party start negotiating against themselves.

Here's another way to turn silence to your advantage. Remember "Flinch, Reflect, Go silent?" This method is similar. The well-known salesman Zig Ziglar demonstrated the power of silence to handle objections about price. If a potential customer said, "The price is too high," Ziglar would respond by asking, "The price is too high?" and then biting his lip. By turning the objection into a question and then remaining silent, he could create immense pressure on the customer. Often, they would overcome the objection on their own.

The next time you're in a sales situation or involved in an important negotiation, think about biting your tongue and staying quiet. Not only will you gather more information, but you might also achieve a better result.

REAL LIFE NEGOTIATION—JIM: In one case, someone was eager to buy an instrumentation company I was selling, but whenever he asked me a question, my brief silence made him nervous, and he started talking again. He was a chatty guy and hated silence. He began to offer more money and change the terms of the deal because my silence led him to believe I didn't like what he had to say about the offer. However, the truth was that he couldn't stay quiet long enough to get a response, and I was patient enough to wait him out. In the end, he negotiated a worse deal than he might have if he had stopped talking for a moment. Similarly, great journalists and detectives also leverage the power of silence in their interviews, especially when they want to get someone to share something they might not otherwise say. Just by remaining silent, they create pressure on their interview subject to fill that awkward pause.

7. MAKE ROOM FOR HUMOR

When you think of negotiation, you probably imagine a serious and intense discussion—two sides sitting across from each other, presenting their strongest arguments, and battling for the deal they want. While it's true that negotiations can be challenging, they don't always have to be so serious. Using humor in conversations can be a powerful way to break the ice, build rapport, and even help you secure a better deal.

That's because humor is more than just making people laugh; it's a way to build connections, ease tension, and foster trust between people. When individuals laugh together, it creates rapport and helps them feel more at ease with each other.

Using humor in a negotiation is like adding seasoning to a dish—you don't want too much, and you must sprinkle it in at the right moments. Starting a negotiation with a lighthearted comment or a joke can set a positive tone for the discussion. It can help both sides relax and create a more comfortable atmosphere. For example, if you're negotiating with a new client, you could say, "I've been looking forward to this meeting... but only because it means I don't have to work spreadsheets until my eyes glaze over anymore!"

Humor can also go a long way when things become tense or uncomfortable. A well-timed joke can help diffuse the situation. For example, during one negotiation for a business, we aimed for a $1 million concession on the price. Our negotiator joked by putting his pinkie to the corner of his mouth like Dr. Evil and said we wanted "One MILLION dollars." Everyone cracked up, and we secured the concession.

While humor can be effective, it's essential to be careful with how you use it. Here are some guidelines to help you strike the right balance:

- **Know Your Audience:** Not everyone responds to humor in the same way. Before using humor, try to gauge the personality of the person or group you're negotiating with. You might want to dial it back if they seem very formal or serious. But if they're more relaxed, feel free to lighten the mood with a joke or two.

- **Keep it Professional:** Humor in a negotiation should always be appropriate and respectful. Avoid jokes that could be perceived as rude or unprofessional, or that touch on sensitive topics such as politics or personal issues. Stick to light, noncontroversial humor that's easy to understand.

- **Don't Overdo It:** Too much humor can make you seem like you're not taking the negotiation seriously. You want to be funny, but not at the expense of professionalism. A few well-placed jokes or lighthearted comments can do wonders but don't turn the entire negotiation into a comedy show.

- **Use Self-Deprecation Sparingly:** A little self-deprecating humor can make you seem more approachable but overdoing it can undermine your authority or credibility. For example, you could say something like, "I'm not a math genius, but even I can see these numbers look good," to make a point without taking yourself too seriously. It can be particularly effective when you are in a superior position in the organization or life—humor equalizes people.

Remember, negotiation isn't just about getting what you want; it's about creating an environment where both sides can reach a mutually beneficial agreement. And sometimes, all it takes is a little laugh to get there.

REAL LIFE NEGOTIATION—ONYI: People connect best with those they like. I enjoy making others laugh and feel at ease, and I like to build relationships even before a deal is on the table. Many deals start because people come to me first because they don't like my competitor, whom they see as an emotionless corporation, while I have personality and am highly relatable. Building these relationships is essential to laying the groundwork for future deals.

WHAT YOU DO BEFORE THE DEAL MATTERS MOST

As you've seen in this chapter, smart negotiation combines preparation, timing, psychology, and practice. Whether you're mastering the art of the flinch, listening more than you speak, or using humor to build rapport, the tactics you choose can influence the outcome—and the relationship that follows.

However, even the best tactics won't save you if you arrive unprepared.

Before entering any negotiation, you need to understand your position, define your walkaway point, know what the other side values, and map out your potential trade-offs. In the next chapter, we'll explore the essential steps to prepare for a negotiation—because great negotiators don't wing it. They get ready. Let's dig in.

〉 CHAPTER THREE TAKEAWAYS 〈

1. **Use frameworks like "Tell, Ask, Connect, Sell."** Building rapport and trust before pitching dramatically increases your chances of success.

2. **Master silence.** Strategic silence, especially when paired with flinching and reflection, can prompt your counterpart to concede or reveal more.

3. **Anchor early and wisely.** Setting the first number (with confidence and data) shifts the negotiation in your favor, even if you ultimately concede.

NEGOTIATION TACTICS TO AVOID

EVERYONE ASPIRES TO BE a great negotiator. We research tactics, practice our arguments, and aim for the best possible results. But equally important is understanding what to avoid, as well as knowing what to do. Some of the biggest negotiation mistakes aren't about saying the wrong thing—they're about habits, shortcuts, and pressure-driven behaviors that quietly harm deals and relationships.

In this chapter, we examine eight common traps that even experienced negotiators can fall into. From the temptation to force a deal, to the pressure of artificial deadlines, to the urge to "nibble" at the last minute—these behaviors might win a battle but lose the war. We'll share stories of what happens when these tactics backfire and how to avoid them in your own deals.

Think of this as your negotiation "anti-playbook." Avoiding these mistakes will give you an advantage and increase your chances to build trust, reach an agreement, and secure a long-term deal.

Let's explore seven Negotiation "Don'ts" to avoid.

LET PERFECT BE THE ENEMY OF GOOD

We've all been trained for most of our lives to get the best deal possible, and that makes sense most of the time. It's easy to find the best deal on a car or TV because we can research every detail, and there's no good reason to pay more or get less.

However, you may need to change your mindset when it comes to other high-stakes negotiations, such as buying or selling a business. Sometimes, you should make a deal even if there's a chance to find a better one later. If the deal is close enough, take it. Why? Because in situations like these, if there's money on the table, it makes sense to take it. Let us explain.

If you are thinking about selling your company, you must accept that the future is uncertain. That's why, if someone offers you 95% of what you're aiming for, you might want to go ahead and close the deal instead of pushing for that extra 5%. Why? Because you don't know when or even if another buyer will come along or if your business could face disruptions that could harm its value.

Removing money from the table can also lead to significant long-term wins. I worked with a CEO, Wayne, who successfully recapitalized his business four times over a 20-year period. Each time, Wayne brought in new money into his business, bought out the old money, and took some money off the table for himself—all while retaining an equity position in the industry. He was so good at this that we eventually referred to this as "Wayne's Rule."

There's another strong reason to find ways to remove money from the table: you'll play more freely. Professional athletes who play sports like golf or baseball know that the looser their grip on the club or bat, the faster and more forcefully they can swing and achieve results. That's why clubs and bats sometimes fly into the crowd. These players also realize that they tighten up and underperform if they clutch too tightly.

The same is true for high-stakes negotiations. You'll get fewer desirable outcomes if you're too tense and nervous. Entrepreneurs are risk-takers, but we rarely like to have all our chips on the table at once. When you take money off the table, you'll play more freely because there is less risk attached to each decision and action you take. You'll be a better leader as a result.

That's why, when you find yourself in situations where you can take money off the table, look for opportunities to say yes instead of striving to make the absolute best deal ever. Your goal should be to get it close enough. When you do that, you'll find that you'll come out much further ahead in the long run.

USE FORCE TO GET YOUR WAY

Anyone who has ever been in a healthy relationship intuitively understands that forcing people to do something isn't a recipe for sustainable success. While you might get someone to change in the short term, you'll eventually have to pay the price for that decision.

The same principle applies in business. I often see leaders fall into this trap. They assert their authority to force others to comply, then wonder why it all fails. Whenever you use force to achieve a goal, almost a universal law of physics kicks in: there is an equal and opposite reaction.

Negotiations should follow this principle if you want your relationships—and your success—to last. When making a deal with someone, you have every reason to ensure it's a win-win for both sides. If you try to force an agreement to gain an advantage, the other party will do everything possible to counterbalance the situation by screwing you over in another part of the deal.

We aren't saying that one shouldn't advocate their position confidently, but seeking an advantage in every situation leads to unbalanced deals. My experience shows that real magic happens when both parties feel it's a win-win, where everyone believes they're gaining something positive from the deal. The energy is positive, and the parties are more willing to work together.

REAL LIFE NEGOTIATION—JIM: Consider an example from a company Jim was working with when a key employee left. The leadership worried that this person might start their own business and compete. The employee had never signed a non-compete agreement with the company, but that didn't stop them from doing everything they could to force him to sign one now. They didn't realize that they had zero leverage and yet continued to up the pressure.

Big mistake. Since this employee was not motivated to sign such an agreement, they quickly became upset and transformed from a potential partner who could have helped sell their product—into a genuine competitor determined to beat them in the market.

Instead of seeking a win-win situation where both the company and the employee could benefit, they chose to alienate him, ensuring he would promote their competitor's products instead of theirs. They had already lost, and the best move was to lean in and create a friend (not that they had a choice).

One of my favorite quotes is, "If you are being run out of town, pick up a baton and lead the parade."

REAL LIFE NEGOTIATION—ONYI: I had a competitor with a very similar name who wanted to explore a potential merger. I considered it because it made sense as a strategic move and partnership. The problem was that the other company had 29 locations at the time, while we only had 14. As a result, they felt like they were the dominant players and should lead the process. I knew we had a stronger infrastructure and better system, but they had more locations and a more recognizable name.

My brand focuses on providing customers with the best experience at the best price and making things as affordable as possible for franchisees. The other CEO was older and used his brand more to make quick money, up charging equipment and products to his franchisees so he could profit while offering them little to no support.

This difference in management and opinion—and the other CEO's perspective that it was his show—ended the deal. Five years later, we had grown 200X and their stores had dwindled down to 20.

BE CHRONICALLY LATE

English writer Edward Verrall Lucas wrote, "I have noticed that the people who are late are often so much jollier than the people who have to wait for them." Now, we realize most of us have been late for something more than once—sometimes it can't be helped. In such cases, simply call your host (or the other party) and explain the situation. Usually, it works out fine.

But what we want to focus on here is the message that habitual lateness sends to others. Essentially, it shows that our time is less important than yours. This is not how to begin a negotiation based on trust and understanding.

Think about how you feel whenever you go to the doctor's office, or even the DMV, where you think you have an appointment—but you find yourself waiting 15 minutes, a half hour, or even longer before you talk to someone. It's incredibly frustrating. That's because you feel like you're wasting your valuable time and that the other person and organization is demonstrating that their time is more valuable than yours.

Unfortunately, this is a common practice, especially among service companies, that seem to overlook how damaging it can be to build lasting customer relationships. At a minimum, an effort should be made to explain the reason for the meeting delay. Otherwise, why would a customer want to work with you if you don't value their time?

If being late is a habit, it's best to break it now. Otherwise, you risk insulting all your friends and business associates, and it might even sink a critical negotiation.

REAL LIFE NEGOTIATION—ONYI: While showing up on time is a critical way to both demonstrate and earn respect, so is upholding your end of a bargain on time.

One thing that has helped my business is that I am never late paying bills to my landlords, vendors, or banks. I have been able to maintain the best prices and relationships with my staff and vendors in my general contracting company because I can be expected to pay for services immediately. Most larger companies pay on net 30 terms, but I know that my guys hate that, so I make a point to make online payments within the hour of receiving an invoice. This allows me to get the best possible prices from my vendors because they know they can make more from another general contractor, but I pay quickly, and a lot of times, speed is better to them because they have to float their employees' pay while waiting for other companies to pay them finally.

FALL INTO THE "HIGHER AUTHORITY" TRAP

There is a technique called "Higher Authority" that many people use to gain an advantage in negotiation. This involves reaching an agreement with the person you're negotiating with directly, then bringing in someone above you who has the actual authority to approve or reject the deal.

Anyone who has bought a car at a dealership has experienced this. When you decide to buy the car, you sit down at the salesperson's desk to negotiate the price. After some back and forth, the salesperson says they need to talk to their manager before agreeing on that price.

You know what happens next. The salesperson walks away to find their boss—and who knows what they actually discuss whether it's the terms of the deal or last night's game—and then walks back in, shaking their head. "Sorry, my boss says we can't do that price," he says. "But we can do this instead." Inevitably, that price is higher than the one you had already agreed to. It's frustrating, but what can you do?

Using "higher authority" in negotiations can be effective, but it certainly doesn't help build trust or long-term relationships. Still, we see this tactic used frequently in the business world. So, how can you counter this approach?

Whenever you enter a negotiation, establish the ground rules right away by asking the person you're working with whether they have decision-making authority. Ask, "If we agree today, do you have the authority to sign the deal?"

If the person says no, they're authorized to negotiate but cannot agree to the deal, then it's time to pause. Let the other person know you're not interested in negotiating further until the people who can say yes to the deal get involved. If they are unwilling, you know it's time to step back entirely. They're not interested in negotiating in good faith.

When someone refuses to involve the decision-maker in the negotiation, you can count on one thing: that other person will want an additional concession in the deal. I speak from experience. When the person I'm negotiating with doesn't have the final say on a deal, I've learned to hold something back—not revealing everything during the negotiation—because I know that, whenever the Higher Authority gets involved, they'll want something extra.

The Higher Authority as a negotiating tactic is powerful, but you need to be careful how you use it if you choose to use it. If you dislike it when it's used against you, you can be sure others feel the same way.

THE "GET 'EM WHILE THEY'RE HOT" TRAP

We've all experienced walking down a city street and hearing a food vendor call out to "get 'em while they're hot!" It's an effective sales tactic because it creates a sense of urgency. However, there are many times when someone might generate a false sense of urgency to close a deal, perhaps by citing company policy or random accounting deadlines.

For instance, Jim knows a CEO who constantly sets artificial deadlines, claiming that if his team doesn't improve by February, he will fire everyone. However, setting these kinds of self-imposed and arbitrary deadlines rarely produces the results he or others like him are aiming for. The fact that the threats are empty causes everyone to ignore them.

In negotiations, it's important to recognize how the other party might exploit artificial time pressure to pressure you into signing a bad deal.

One way to gauge if the time pressure in a deal is genuine is to flip the script on the other party by asking, "What happens if we go past the deadline?" The response you receive will reveal a lot about whether the deadline was real and if you can now adjust the timeline to your advantage.

Sometimes, it's not the other party putting artificial pressure on a deal—it's you.

REAL LIFE NEGOTIATION—JIM: I tried to buy a small instrumentation company earlier in my career. Both sides agreed on a strong set of terms, but then I got major surprise when I got an unsolicited offer to sell the company I was running to a much larger firm for a great price. I knew the owners couldn't pass up that deal.

I knew I couldn't manage both deals at once, but I worried that delaying the acquisition of the instrumentation company might cause another firm to swoop in and grab it. I compared waiting to parking my car in a rough neighborhood with the keys in the ignition, open for anyone to drive off.

But I still chose to take things one step at a time. I completed the deal to sell my company, and a few months later, I revisited that instrumentation company. And guess what happened? They were still willing to negotiate on the same terms we had previously agreed upon. Sometimes, time isn't a factor. Recognizing genuine and fake deadlines is a crucial skill for any good negotiator. Ultimately, our goal in any negotiation should be to secure the best deal, not the fastest one.

GIVE ON PRICE WITHOUT TAKING AWAY VALUE

Anytime you're selling or negotiating, you're trying to balance the price you're asking for with the value you're providing. If you want to get the highest price possible, you aim to convince your customers of the value they're getting in exchange.

But we've all faced situations where the other party insists on paying less than your asking price. That can be challenging, especially when you're offering high-end, premium products or services, and you deal with a client who wants all the bells and whistles but is only willing to pay a discounted rate.

You have two strategies you can consider:

If you face a highly price-sensitive client who won't pay your asking price, it may be best to turn them away entirely — even though that can be difficult. This is particularly true if the client asks you to quote a price where you might lose money.

On the other hand, if you need to close a deal for various reasons, such as trying to meet your sales targets, consider another strategy. You can offer your customer a lower price, but you should reduce some of the value in return. For example, if your product includes both pre- and post-installation services, and the customer wants a lower price, give it to them but inform them they won't receive the installation services as part of the deal.

Their reaction will reveal a lot. You'll often notice they want those additional services, which motivates them to pay the full price.

Certainly, one of the key roles in a negotiation like this is to determine what value can be sacrificed at any point without damaging the customer's experience. But how do you decide which features or services to remove to offset the lower price?

Think of a naval captain as an analogy. Naturally, every

ship sustains some damage during its journey—losing some value, to keep our analogy consistent. One method captains use to assess how serious a loss might be is by asking if the damage is above or below the water line.

If something goes wrong above the water line—such as a winch failure or a toaster explosion in the mess hall—things that don't threaten the ship's sinking—then the captain understands it's not a critical issue. It can be addressed later or even delegated to a subordinate to resolve. Or, in a negotiation, that's a feature or service you can remove to give the customer the lower price they're requesting.

But suppose any problem is below the water line, meaning it threatens the seaworthiness of the craft and the safety of the crew. That's not a feature you can remove without jeopardizing the core of what you're selling. It's a fine line, right? You want to remove enough value to justify the lower price, but if you take away too much, the customer will have a bad experience and won't want to do business with you again. Water is coming into the ship; if it isn't stopped, you are heading to the bottom.

Applying this to negotiations more broadly, sometimes the concession the other party asks for is above the water line, meaning you can afford to make a sacrifice. But you need to stand firm when they request concessions that are below the water line.

REAL LIFE NEGOTIATION—ONYI: I'm not a fan of doing

specials, and I tell my franchisees and marketing department that. I'd rather give something away for free than offer a discount. My view is that if we run specials, people will wait for discounts and often assume we're open to negotiation when we're not.

We aim to be the best in our industry and have been recognized many times for it. We're also the fastest-growing franchise in our field, but why? We offer excellent service and atmosphere at competitive prices. This approach works for us—if our prices are a third of what our biggest competitors charge, with similar value, why do we feel the need to offer discounts? If someone expects a discount, we're probably not the right place for them, and that's okay. My philosophy is that not all money is good money.

On the other hand, if you need to close a deal for reasons like trying to meet your sales targets, consider another approach. You can offer your customer a lower price, but you should reduce some of the value in exchange. For example, if your product includes both pre- and post-installation services, and the customer wants a lower price, give it to them but inform them they won't receive the installation services as part of the deal.

LET NIBBLES RUIN THE NEGOTIATION

One common technique is what Jim likes to call "The Nibble." This happens when you've already shaken hands to close a deal, and just as you're about to sign the papers, the other side tries to get one last concession.

It can drive you nuts.

One of the common places where you'll see the Nibble used is in car dealerships. You spend time with the salespeople, asking questions and test-driving cars before going to their desks to discuss the numbers. Then, after you think you've agreed on a price, they bring up some extra fees—like for the floor mats or the undercoating. And it always comes up at the last minute.

Another place you might see something like this is when you shop at a big box retail store. Let's say you're buying a TV, and as the cashier rings you up, they try to get you to buy the extended warranty or maintenance insurance. There is a reason for this—retailers make most of their profit on these add-ons at the last minute.

But Nibbles can be even more sneaky. You might agree to a deal only to discover that some extra items or fees you never discussed appear in the fine print of your agreement.

We've all experienced it—and no one likes it. So why do people try to use the Nibble at all?

First, the Nibbles are highly profitable extras that give them a little bonus. Second, the strategy of deploying the Nibble is that your emotional barriers are lowered. You thought you already had a deal, so you're more likely to agree to whatever the extra ask is to push things through.

Indeed, doing this definitely tests some ethical boundaries.

And it often leaves a bad taste in someone's mouth, making it unlikely they will do business with you again. But it can get you what you want.

The good news is that there are also ways you can counter the Nibble.

The most important thing to remember is that both you and the party you're negotiating with feel some pressure to close the deal. While you might want that car or new TV, you must realize that the seller also wants you to buy it. This gives you more leverage than you might think. Here are a couple of actions you can consider when you encounter the Nibble:

- **Use Humor:** This is my favorite approach. I'll laugh if I catch someone trying to get a Nibble out of me. Then I say, "You're not serious, are you? You're willing to blow this deal over a few extra dollars?" After that, I zip my lips and let the silence work for me. This method will shut down the Nibble six times out of ten.
- **Call Their Bluff:** The other option is simply standing up and heading for the door. You could even say, "I deal from integrity, and I thought we had a deal. Either you cross that item off the agreement, or I'm leaving." Yes, there might be some sunk costs if this doesn't work in your favor, but you will also find that no competent salesperson will let someone ready to sign an agreement walk out the door over a minor Nibble worth a few hundred bucks.

While the Nibble is used frequently in negotiations, we advise you to be cautious about overusing it or using it in the wrong situation. Although it can help you get what you want once, it might turn the other person off so much that you'll never make a deal with them again. The good news is that if you find the Nibble being used against you, you will have some options to defend against it effectively.

REAL LIFE NEGOTIATION—ONYI: Sometimes my vendors try to nibble, offering us something we want but then attempting to get something they want in return. When negotiating, I prefer having someone I report to or speak for so that if things go sideways, I can say, "Let me talk to XYZ." (Of course, whoever I am negotiating with knows that I have the authority to make decisions, so they understand they can negotiate with me, but I also have someone to fall back on for certain issues.)

When I work with my vendors, my go-to people are my franchisees because I am technically negotiating on their behalf, not just my own. This usually works well because I can portray myself as the hero by saying I convinced them or as the villain if I suggest they aren't willing to cooperate, emphasizing that I need the vendor to work with me to achieve a result that makes everyone happy. Then, the person feels like it's me and them working together to close the deal with the franchisees. This is a good example of using higher authority to leverage influence and counter the Nibble.

GET READY FOR THE REAL DEAL

A successful negotiation is not just about what you say; it's also about what you resist. Resisting the impulse to dominate, rush, or overreach is key. Avoiding the traps we've discussed here is what separates dealmakers from dealbreakers.

But knowing what not to do isn't the same as knowing how to succeed. In the next chapter, we'll shift from mistakes to effective strategies: how to handle tough negotiators, close strongly, and—when necessary—walk away on your own terms. Once you've avoided the errors, it's time to bring your best tactics to the table.

> ## ⟩　CHAPTER FOUR TAKEAWAYS　⟨

1. **Don't nibble or overreach.** Small last-minute asks ("nibbling") can damage trust, while aggressive tactics risk alienating the other side.

2. **Avoid chasing perfection.** Trying to win every point can backfire—sometimes "good enough" is the best outcome.

3. **Don't get too clever.** Overuse of tricks or overly complex maneuvers can undermine credibility and derail negotiations.

CLOSING THE DEAL: NEGOTIATION TACTICS IN ACTION

YOU'VE BUILT RAPPORT, UNCOVERED interests, and made your case. Now comes the moment of truth: closing the deal. This is where negotiation moves from theory to action—where people's true motivations, emotions, and values are revealed. Some deals fall apart at the last minute, not because of logic, but because of personalities, pressure, or poorly timed comments.

In this chapter, we'll explore how to navigate the final moments of a negotiation when things can either come together beautifully or unravel entirely. From handling hardball opponents to recognizing when to walk away from a toxic relationship, we'll share tactics and stories that reveal how experienced negotiators close with clarity, ethics, and grace.

You'll learn how to identify hidden motivations, deal with difficult or unethical people, and—perhaps most importantly—how to stay quiet when silence is the smartest move.

Negotiation isn't just about signing on the dotted line. It's successful when both sides leave the table with mutual respect and confidence that they made a good deal. Let's get started.

HANDLING TOUGH NEGOTIATORS

Every now and then, you'll encounter a tough negotiator, someone who plays hardball and won't give in easily. We'll explore some strategies to handle these opponents effectively, but the most important thing to remember is: staying calm and sticking to your strategy is key to navigating these situations. Keep the conversation focused on the facts and the benefits for both sides. If things start to get too heated, don't hesitate to suggest a break.

Here's a negotiation secret: No one is truly illogical. It has taken Jim years to realize this because it frustrates him when someone asks for something that seems completely unreasonable or cancels the deal for reasons that don't make sense. They seem entirely irrational, and as an engineer, he struggles to connect with someone who doesn't appear to be acting rationally.

However, Jim has come to realize that no one is illogical. The key is understanding what influences their priorities and how they see the world. Once you understand that, everything changes.

So, if the negotiation begins to feel difficult, your first question should be what information you might be missing. Once you understand what's important to them, you'll know what you can offer in the negotiation that they value and that you value far less.

One example is knowing someone's upbringing and the circumstances of their youth. If someone grew up poor and without money, that could continue to influence their actions and decisions as an adult. Suppose you're negotiating with someone like this, and all they seem to focus on is the amount of money they will receive in the deal, seemingly overlooking other beneficial terms they might receive. This might seem irrational at first. You might even think they are just greedy. But when you consider the circumstances of their childhood as context, it all makes sense. They continue to be driven by the lower rungs of Maslow's Hierarchy of Needs. They are money-oriented because they never want to experience poverty again.

If you're negotiating with someone like this, it might offer you the chance to gain something else—like better terms— in exchange for giving up some money. As we've seen, an intelligent negotiator can make the headline price look great and win the negotiation regarding the terms and timing of the payments.

Another reason someone might act in ways that seem illogical is when they are highly image-conscious. These are people who worry about how others perceive them. They show up with tailored suits, expensive watches, and luxury vehicles. If you're negotiating with someone like this, it might be crucial for them to be seen as "winning" the deal. You might have a perfect deal on the table, but if they don't think others will see them as having the upper hand, you're unlikely to close the deal.

This can be a tough obstacle to overcome, but it creates an opportunity to appear as if they have won the deal even when they haven't. For example, the merged firm might keep their company name, but you'll pay a lower price and keep full operational control.

Another area to watch is when people are affiliation-driven. They might not care whether the deal is good or bad, as long as the "right" kind of people approve of it. These individuals ask for your references and check to see if you've worked with people they like and respect. An example of this would be agreeing to a poor financial deal just to get involved with a company founded by a celebrity.

Another factor that can trigger "irrational" behavior in negotiations is a focus on power—especially political power. People might become obsessed with obtaining a prestigious title and having many reports under them. They might even accept a lower salary to gain that type of power—which you can use to your advantage if necessary. This is how we end up with executive senior vice presidents who don't earn much money.

Next time you encounter someone who seems irrational, pause. Step back, think about what might motivate their actions, and ask questions. If you understand that, you could find a way to make a deal that works better for you.

AVOIDING UNETHICAL NEGOTIATORS

Of course, the issue might not be resolved simply by identifying the correct logic. Instead, it could be about ethics. While Jim has found that most (about 99%) of the businesspeople he has known throughout his career are exceptionally ethical and moral—they understand that treating people fairly and honestly is the best way to build long-lasting and sustainable relationships—there are some exceptions.

There are unethical businesspeople out there, who treat people as part of a transaction and may not care as much about doing things correctly if it compromises the "win." None of us wants to be taken advantage of or forced to deal with someone unethical in some way. So, how do we know what signs to watch for?

Based on my experience, there is one simple red flag that every unethical person shares: they are the ones who accuse everyone else of being dishonest.

Throughout his career as a leader, Jim has always believed in the hypothesis of *"lead with trust."* In other words, he initially trusted everyone until they proved him wrong. But the alarm bells should start going off anytime you meet someone approaching a relationship with the fear of being taken advantage of by everyone around them. Why? Because that's the first sign that they want to take advantage of *you*—they think this way, so they assume others do, too —and they want to be sure they can screw you over before you have a chance to do the same to them.

REAL LIFE NEGOTIATION—JIM: When a potential client contacted me, and the first question he asked was, "How do I know you won't screw me?" I'll admit, I was taken aback. Of course, I wasn't out to take advantage of him. And I certainly would do anything he asked to make him feel more comfortable about setting the terms of our working arrangement if it was good for me, too.

But I also believe that people with high levels of integrity don't worry about being taken advantage of. His primary concern was covering himself, which was an immediate red flag for me, so I turned down his business. If you're wondering if someone you might want to work with is ethical, look for the simple sign of whether they're apprehensive about being taken advantage of. It means they'll look for the chance to take advantage of you instead.

REMEMBER THAT ALL RELATIONSHIPS ARE VOLUNTARY

If all of your rationalizing and best efforts to further the negotiation fail—or if you get the sense you're dealing with an unethical opponent, then this may not be a deal you want to pursue after all. The key to breaking free from an unhappy relationship is recognizing that all relationships are voluntary. This is especially true in negotiations.

Many of us have been there before where you have an impossible boss, employee, or even customer who continues violating your rights. Even when you try to establish boundaries, they continue to violate them. The key to breaking free from these kinds of relationships is to remember that they are voluntary and that you are the one who is opting into continuing them. Abuse in relationships begins with the consent of the victim if you stick around. In other words, no matter how much you think you need that deal or that job or that customer, you are the one consenting to being abused by staying. And that's something you can change. Remember, life is short, and you have more power to change than you might think.

Jim remembers working with a coaching client who operated in the meetings and event space. His client had a customer who represented the bulk of his revenue and drove him crazy by pushing down prices. Jim's client recognized that his market space was becoming increasingly commoditized. While he offered excellent customer service and high-touch events, he had begun to lose money because his customer wouldn't allow him to get his prices for his phenomenal service. No matter how much he tried to explain and negotiate, his customer wouldn't budge. So, ultimately, my client decided he had to close that part of his business down and fire his customer. But guess what happened next? His customer then begged him to return and continue working with them. Fortunately, my client had firmly decided to walk away and invest his time and resources in a much more profitable aspect of his business where his other customers were willing to pay him fairly for his services.

The critical point is that you probably have more options than you think. That's why, when you're feeling beaten up by a relationship you don't think you can afford to lose, think again. Remember that every relationship is voluntary, and you shouldn't accept any less than you deserve. Don't let yourself suffer abuse—take control of your happiness.

ENDING THE NEGOTIATION WELL

We talked earlier about how you can leverage the power of silence in a negotiation, and there is no time when it is more important to stop talking—to zip your lips or swallow your tongue—than when you and the other side have come to a deal. The temptation, of course, is to keep talking—to rave about what a great deal this is or show the other side how much value they're getting at these terms.

If you find yourself in this situation, we advise you: Stop. Talking.

REAL LIFE NEGOTIATION—JIM: I recall a time when I watched a salesperson in action selling large, expensive pieces of capital equipment we created for the utility industry. This salesperson was brilliant—they really nailed it. The client sat there in awe and wonder. They were ready to sign anything we presented to them.

But you can guess what happened?

Yes, the salesperson kept talking and talking and talking. During their presentation, they started bragging about how effective the pumps are inside the equipment we sell. They kept going until the customer finally spoke up and interrupted them. "We've had tremendous problems with those pumps," they said. "If you use those pumps, we have a major problem."

Uh oh.

I watched the salesperson's face shift from utter confidence to panic. What seemed like a sure thing had just become a disaster.

Any sales or negotiation discussion aims to provide enough information for your client to make an informed decision and close a deal. You don't need anything more than that. You can only lose when you stretch things out from there.

Maybe you've been in a similar situation where you stayed up all night working on a PowerPoint to pitch your boss your great new idea. You're proud of all the effort you put into it—despite the sacrifices it required.

When the big moment arrives, you nail it—your boss is nodding their head and might even start to smile a bit. They listen and quickly thumb through the impressive deck you created. They might even stand up and say, "Impressive work; when can we start?" You've got the deal!

You've won. As much work as you put into the

presentation—there's no need to show your work, even if you have 30 more slides to share. It's time to shut up and celebrate.

One of the rules that my sales team and I have developed to deal with situations like these is that when the other side says "okay," the only appropriate response is, "Who wants lunch? I'm buying!"

That phrase "Who wants lunch?" became a signal for everyone on my executive team when they had agreement and it was time to stop talking.

The lesson was clear for everyone: bite your lip and stop talking once you get the deal.

DON'T GLOAT

Negotiation can be intense, and it's easy to feel a rush of excitement or even pride when you walk away with a win. However, experienced business negotiators know that what you do at the end of a negotiation can have a lasting impact. No matter how well it went for you, there are good reasons why you should never gloat or brag. Instead, if you must speak, it's wise to compliment the other side for their negotiation skills. Here's why.

1. PRESERVE PROFESSIONAL RELATIONSHIPS

In business, the relationships you form are often just as important as the deals you close. Gloating after a negotiation might seem minor, but it can harm these relationships. When you celebrate your success too openly, the other party could feel embarrassed, disappointed, or even resentful. A little empathy goes a long way. You never know when you'll need to work with this person or company again, so ending on a positive note can keep that door open.

For example, imagine you just negotiated a big contract with a supplier. You got a great price and the exact terms you wanted. Now, if you walk away acting like you "won," that supplier might feel undervalued or disrespected. In the future, if you need better terms or a quicker turnaround, the supplier might not be as motivated to help. However, by showing respect and avoiding gloating, you signal that you value the partnership beyond just this one deal.

2. KEEP YOUR REPUTATION INTACT

In business, reputation is everything. Word spreads quickly in any industry, and if people hear that you are a gracious negotiator, they're more likely to approach you for future deals. Conversely, if they hear that you gloated or rubbed in a successful negotiation, they might avoid working with you. They may fear you'll treat them the same way or that you'll be difficult to negotiate with.

Thanking the other side for their effort or complimenting their negotiation skills can leave a lasting positive impression. Even if the outcome wasn't in their favor, they'll remember that you treated them with respect. This approach can also boost your credibility. People appreciate dealing with those who are fair and respectful, even in competitive situations.

3. BUILD TRUST FOR FUTURE DEALS

Ending a negotiation respectfully builds trust. This matters because negotiations often have multiple rounds. There could be new terms, renewals, or changes over time. If you gloat, the other side might trust you less in the future. They might even try to "get even" in the next negotiation, which could result in tougher terms for you.

For example, if you're negotiating a contract with a supplier for the first time, they're probably already testing the waters to see what kind of partner you'll be. If you show respect and appreciation, they're more likely to trust you over time. Trust can make future negotiations easier and faster, as both sides understand they're dealing with someone who will handle the situation professionally.

4. SHOW EMOTIONAL INTELLIGENCE

A key trait of a great negotiator is emotional intelligence. This involves understanding how others feel and responding in a way that considers those emotions. People often work hard to prepare for negotiations, and it's natural for them to feel disappointed if they don't get exactly what they wanted. Recognizing and respecting that can make a big difference.

Saying something like, "I really appreciate how well you

handled this negotiation," shows empathy. This simple recognition can ease any frustration they might feel and give them a sense of pride. When people feel respected, they're more likely to respect you back.

5. MAINTAIN A POSITIVE MINDSET

Gloating can cause unnecessary negativity. Approaching negotiations with humility and respect helps you stay positive, which benefits both sides. Ending on a good note lets everyone walk away feeling it was a productive and respectful experience.

Remember, business negotiations aren't just about "winning" or "losing." They're about finding common ground and creating mutual value. When both sides feel they were treated fairly, it sets the stage for positive future interactions. No one wants to do business with someone who makes them feel like they lost.

6. COMPLIMENT THE OTHER SIDE'S SKILLS

Instead of gloating, use the chance to compliment the other side's skills. A simple phrase, such as "You're a tough negotiator" or "I admire your approach," can make a big difference. It shows you recognize their effort and skill, even if the outcome favored you.

Complimenting the other side also boosts their confidence. This might seem counterintuitive but consider this:

confident negotiators are often more willing to work with you again. They won't shy away from negotiating because they feel they did well, even if they didn't get exactly what they wanted. By recognizing their strengths, you make it easier to engage with them in future negotiations.

Ultimately, a good negotiator understands that it's about more than just the terms on paper. It's about building lasting professional relationships, protecting your reputation, and ensuring that both parties feel respected. Gloating at the end of a negotiation might bring a short-term sense of satisfaction, but it can lead to long-term consequences.

So, the next time you walk away from a successful negotiation, remember to stay humble. Thank the other side for their effort, recognize their skills, and leave the door open for future talks.

And, most importantly, invite them to lunch.

AFTER THE HANDSHAKE

Ending a negotiation well is just as important as how you start. A respectful closing—free of gloating and full of gratitude—sets the tone for future conversations and leaves a lasting impression. Because here's the truth: no deal happens in a vacuum. People remember how you made them feel. And if you want a reputation as someone others want to do business with again, you have to finish with finesse.

But the end of a negotiation is really just the start of something new.

What happens next—the post-deal phase—is where all your planning, promises, and paperwork face reality. How do you ensure the deal actually delivers? What steps do you take if the other party starts to deviate from the agreed terms? And how do you turn a successful negotiation into a long-term relationship?

In the next chapter, we'll cover what happens after the handshake: how to follow through, stay aligned, and ensure both sides keep their promises.

⟩ CHAPTER FIVE TAKEAWAYS ⟨

1. **Closing is just the beginning.** Finalizing the terms is the start of implementation—protect your agreement with documentation and follow-up.

2. **Mind the details.** Legal clarity, contract language, and precise expectations reduce risk and set the foundation for long-term success.

3. **Keep the relationship alive.** Even after the deal is signed, proactive communication preserves goodwill and opens the door to future opportunities.

AFTER THE NEGOTIATION

CONGRATULATIONS—YOU JUST CLOSED THE deal. However, if you believe the negotiation ends with the signing of the contract, think again. Once a deal is made, the next step is to follow through on what was agreed upon. This means ensuring that both sides adhere to their commitments and that a clear plan is in place for implementation. Don't just sign the deal and disappear. Keep in touch with the other side to ensure everything is running smoothly. This is especially important for long-term business relationships.

This is where many professionals stumble. They celebrate the win, archive the email chain, and move on to the next opportunity. However, real negotiators understand that closing is merely the beginning. The aftermath of a negotiation is where reputations are built, relationships are strengthened (or damaged), and where the groundwork for your next deal is quietly laid.

In this chapter, we'll guide you through everything that happens after the handshake—from drafting clear term sheets and consulting the right lawyers to protecting yourself with breakup clauses and managing post-deal dynamics. You'll learn how to safeguard your agreement, avoid common pitfalls, and turn one good deal into a long-term strategic advantage.

Because the best negotiators don't just close well—they follow through even better.

BREAKING DOWN A TERM SHEET

So, you've had a successful negotiation, and both sides have agreed on the key terms; now it's time to put everything in writing. This is where a "term sheet" comes into play. A term sheet is a concise, straightforward document that outlines the key terms of your deal before it becomes a formal contract. Think of it as a roadmap for what both sides have agreed to, clearly written so that everyone is on the same page. It's not the final, legally binding contract (that's what the lawyers are for), but it's an important step to prevent any misunderstandings about the deal.

In the world of negotiation, a well-crafted term sheet serves as your safety net. It ensures that both parties understand the details, prevents misunderstandings, and lays a solid foundation for the final contract. By confirming the details in a term sheet, you set the stage for a smooth and successful deal. Here's what the term sheet guarantees:

- **Avoid Misunderstandings:** People can leave the same conversation with different interpretations of what was said. A term sheet makes sure both sides see the exact terms clearly. I even created a term sheet for the negotiation so both parties could review it before we left the room.
- **Establish a Reference Point:** Negotiations can get complicated, and it's easy to miss some details. A term sheet serves as a reference that everyone can consult as the deal progresses.
- **Prepare for Legal Review:** Lawyers appreciate term sheets because they simplify their work. Drafting a contract is much simpler when they have a clear list of agreed-upon terms to follow.
- **Reduce the Risk of Disputes:** If any confusion or disagreements occur later, having a term sheet helps resolve the issue quickly. Both sides can refer to the written agreement to clarify what was initially discussed.

A good term sheet doesn't have to be overly complex, but it must include all the essential parts of the deal. Here's an overview of the key sections you should include:

- **Basic Information:** The names of the involved parties and a brief description of the deal's purpose.

- **Parties:** List both sides' names. If it's a business deal, include the company names and the names of the representatives.

- **Purpose:** Write a one-line statement explaining the purpose of the agreement. For example, "This term sheet outlines the basic terms of the agreement between ABC Corp. and XYZ Ltd. for the sale of 10,000 units of Product A."

- **Key Deal Terms:** This is the core of the term sheet. Here, you'll outline the main terms of the deal. Make sure these deal terms are as clear and detailed as possible. Vague language can lead to confusion later. For example, instead of saying, "Payment due soon after delivery," say, "Payment is due within 30 days after the delivery date." Depending on the negotiation, these could include:

  › *Price:* What is the agreed-upon price or fee? Be specific. If the price includes certain costs (such as shipping or taxes), ensure that's clear as well.

  › *Payment Terms:* How and when will the payment be made? Will it be in installments or a lump sum? Are there any penalties for late payments?

  › *Deliverables:* What does each party agree to provide? For example, if you're selling a product, specify exactly what product will be delivered, how many units, and the deadline.

> *Timeline:* What are the key dates? This may include delivery deadlines, the length of a partnership or agreement, or any milestones that must be met.

- **Contingencies:** Next, you should list any contingencies or conditions that must be fulfilled for the deal to go forward. These are "if-then" statements that protect both parties. Some examples include:
  > *Due Diligence:* "This agreement is contingent upon a satisfactory review of XYZ Ltd.'s financial statements by ABC Corp."
  > *Financing:* "This term sheet depends on XYZ Ltd. securing financing within 60 days."

- **Exclusivity:** Sometimes, you might want to include an exclusivity clause. This is especially crucial when negotiating a significant deal and wanting to ensure the other party isn't seeking better offers elsewhere while finalizing agreements. An exclusivity clause might state, "XYZ Ltd. agrees not to negotiate with other parties regarding the sale of Product A for 90 days while this agreement is being finalized." This provides both sides the confidence that the deal will proceed without outside interference.

- **Confidentiality:** If sensitive information is involved in the negotiation, include a confidentiality clause. This prevents both parties from disclosing deal details to others. This is especially crucial for public companies. At its simplest, the language might state, "Both parties agree to keep the terms of this agreement confidential and not to share them with third parties without the other party's written consent."

- **Termination:** It's a good idea to have a section that outlines how either side can back out of the deal if things go south before a final contract is signed. For example, "Either party may terminate this term sheet upon written notice if a final agreement is not reached within 90 days." This way, if the deal drags on or falls apart, both sides have a clear exit strategy.

While covering all the key points is important, don't make the term sheet overly complicated. It doesn't need to be full of legal jargon or extra details. The goal is to create a document that clearly states the main terms of the deal so everyone understands what's expected.

A good rule of thumb is to ask yourself, "Would someone unfamiliar with this deal be able to read this and understand what's happening?" If the answer is yes, then you're on the right track.

REAL LIFE NEGOTIATION—ONYI: When we lease spaces for franchisees, I review and approve every lease, and we ensure that we get a signed LOI (Letter of Intent) before proceeding. I can't count how many times we've gone to lease, only for the landlord or their attorney to try adding terms we didn't agree to, claiming it's a deal breaker. We always reference the signed LOI, which is then dropped, because we make sure to include all major deal terms in the LOI to prevent this.

Having a deal in writing is always best so you can refer to it later if needed. Misunderstandings can happen between you, your broker, the landlord's broker, and the landlord. Too many people involved in the deal make it crucial to have everything documented, and this rule applies to all deals.

WHY YOU MUST HAVE A BREAKUP CLAUSE

We can't tell you how common it is for business partners to disagree on how to unwind their involvement in the business. Jim estimates that at least 20 percent of the issues he deals with as a CEO Advisor result from the breakup of a business partnership, all of which could have been prevented if they had been planned.

And to some degree, it makes sense: it's almost like asking your new fiancé to sign a prenuptial agreement on your wedding day. Most founders get caught up in the excitement of the moment and figure that they can always work out their problems later. This is a big mistake.

We've seen too many horror stories where partners, many of whom were once close friends, end up despising each other and spending countless dollars on lawyers to try to dissolve their partnership. Equally bad, they jeopardize their companies, their employees' lives, and their customers' well-being by neglecting to establish an agreement before things go wrong.

To avoid these nightmares, do the smart thing and pass up the free business agreement template you can download from the Internet. Instead, hire a competent attorney who is experienced in drafting these types of agreements. Although it may cost you a few thousand dollars upfront, it can save you hundreds of thousands of dollars in the long run.

A reasonable attorney can walk you and your partner or partners through critical questions like:

1. How do you break a deadlock on decisions?
2. How will you value the business during a breakup?
3. How do you decide who buys out who?
4. What powers and rights will the owners have?
5. If owners leave, how will they be paid out, and when? Will it be a lump sum or paid out over time?

Again, working through these questions early might seem like overkill—"We're in love, and we'll be together forever!"—but you need to trust me that this is much easier to resolve now than when you are at each other's throats.

This advice applies to other business agreements, marketing partnerships, joint ventures, and similar arrangements. It's common for interests to diverge over time, and there is usually time to end the arrangement. Ideally, that process is friendly and straightforward rather than nasty, contentious, and costly.

Hopefully, you won't need to use the agreement because things will work out very well. But if they don't, you'll be glad you took the time to get it right from the start.

REAL LIFE NEGOTIATION—JIM: I was working with the two

founders of an entrepreneurial company. Between them, they still owned most of the company. While they had grown the company substantially since its inception, the two partners began to have some serious disagreements about where they wanted the business to go moving forward and how their roles would change as a result. Things had gotten heated when I got involved. The two guys were barely speaking to each other. It seemed clear they were headed for a business divorce.

But when I asked them what provision in their operating agreement laid out how they would break up the company, they looked at me blankly: they didn't have one. We ultimately sold the company, but it was many times harder because there was no preexisting agreement on who got to approve the sale and more importantly, the hundreds of terms.

DON'T FORGET TO INVOLVE YOUR LAWYERS

You'll often need to involve lawyers in formal business deals. (i.e., If the deal involves contracts, intellectual property, or complex terms, having a lawyer review the agreement is a smart move.) While the negotiation mainly occurs between you and the other party, legal professionals can help ensure everything is done correctly and that no loopholes could cause issues.

Many entrepreneurs think that "lawyer" is a general term. They might say, "I need to hire a lawyer." However, the mistake they make is failing to recognize that there are many types of lawyers. Like doctors, most lawyers specialize in a specific area of law to become experts and earn higher pay. When you have a problem, you need to be clear about the kind of lawyer you need to call for help. If you had a problem with your eyes, you wouldn't call a podiatrist; lawyering is the same.

REAL LIFE NEGOTIATION—JIM: I was working with a client trying to buy a company. However, the seller had hired a friend of his, an intellectual property attorney, to assist with the transaction. While this lawyer knew everything about IP, he didn't understand how to handle an acquisition or the key laws and contracts involved. As a result, he ended up costing both sides much more money, headaches, and costly delays, which could have been avoided if the seller had hired a specialist in M&A deals. It is critical to select the right lawyer and get them involved early in the process.

SPECIALIZED ATTORNEYS

Let's look at some of the primary areas of specialization you might need to hire a lawyer to help button up your deal:

1. CORPORATE ATTORNEY

A corporate attorney is a generalist who understands the intricacies of business law, including filings, corporate structures, and certain aspects of tax law. A competent attorney like this can serve as valuable counsel for you in the business and can refer you to a specialist when needed. This is like your family medicine doctor, capable of being broadly knowledgeable but a master of none.

2. EMPLOYMENT LAWYER

Interestingly, approximately half of all court cases involving businesses are related to employment law. It also happens to be one of the areas within your business where you can easily make mistakes and lose your case if you don't have competent representation. This is one area where you need a specialist, even if they cost a bit more. A good employment lawyer can also help draft non-compete employee contracts with clauses that will hold up in your state. Another area where a good employment lawyer can pay for itself is if you are dealing with a labor organization effort inside the business. This is an area where it can be easy to make devastating mistakes if you aren't getting the right advice.

3. IP ATTORNEY

If your business has assets like patents, trademarks, and copyrights, a good intellectual property lawyer can help you maximize your value while protecting them. A reasonable IP attorney can be beneficial when licensing your IP, as they can help write up contracts and other legal constructs to ensure your IP is protected and that you get paid.

4. REAL ESTATE ATTORNEY

Whenever you're buying or leasing property, consulting a top-notch real estate attorney is wise. They understand all aspects of real estate law and can help you secure the best terms for your purchase agreement or lease, including any exit clauses you might need later.

5. FRANCHISE LAWYER

Franchising is a complex area of business law, especially for the franchisor, as it requires understanding the rights of franchisees, who are highly protected. You never want to make promises you can't keep or accidentally violate regulations. A good franchise lawyer can help you navigate the complex system of state and federal laws related to franchising to assist you in successfully expanding your business nationally.

6. M&A ATTORNEY

A company is often the most valuable asset in your portfolio. Therefore, you need expert advice when buying or selling it. You should depend on someone who understands the key issues and can help ensure you not only maximize its value but also have the right protections in place to prevent losses. It turns out there are even specialists within specialists—confident M&A attorneys who focus on specific vertical markets, like pharmaceuticals—bringing an even greater wealth of knowledge and experience to your side.

7. BANKRUPTCY ATTORNEY

This is the call to a lawyer you hope you will never have to make. But the reality is that many entrepreneurs contact a bankruptcy lawyer only when it's already too late. The goal is to find someone who can help you manage your situation in a way that allows you to reorganize or potentially close the business, minimizing risks to you, your shareholders, and your lenders. They can be incredibly helpful in guiding you through to the other side.

Whenever you hire the wrong attorney for a job, they will make mistakes, leading to wasted time, money, and worse outcomes. And that happens more often than it should. So, take the time to understand the issues involved in your deal, and then invest in finding the legal expert most qualified to turn your agreement into a legally binding contract that protects the results you've worked so hard to achieve.

So, where do you start once you engage an attorney? By handing over the term sheet. They'll use this as a guide to draft the final, legally binding contract. Here's what to expect:

1. **Review the Term Sheet with Your Lawyer:** Go over the term sheet with your lawyer to ensure they understand all the details. This will help them identify any

potential legal issues and ensure the contract aligns with your intentions.

2. **Allow for Edits:** Before drafting the contract, your lawyer might recommend revisions or additions to the term sheet. Be open to their advice; they're trained to spot potential risks.

3. **Final Contract Draft:** After both sides' lawyers review the term sheet, they will prepare a final contract. This document will be more detailed and legally binding; however, the basic terms should align with what's outlined in the term sheet.

Now, you might assume that your lawyer's interests fully align with yours, and the right attorney is firmly on your side. However, you should be aware of a few dynamics inherent to the legal profession that could cause their interests to diverge from yours.

The first is revenue motivation. Every lawyer essentially runs their own business, even if they work for a larger firm. In fact, in a big law firm, lawyers are valued based on how much money they generate, either through attracting new clients or by billing their existing clients.

That motivates lawyers to increase their revenue, and there are a few common ways they try to boost their fees. When your lawyers invite colleagues or associates to join a call, you might feel flattered by the extra attention ... until you realize they will be billing you for each person's time. This can be especially frustrating if you're dealing with a senior partner who might ask some of their associates to join the call. They often use these opportunities to mentor younger lawyers, and the partner also earns credit for their billable hours. Like a mother bird, their job is to feed the fledglings.

Another area to watch out for is being billed for "research," which is another way a senior lawyer might try to charge you for training a younger associate. For example, I had an HR contract issue I needed help with a few years ago. I found the best and most experienced lawyer in my state for assistance. However, when I received my bill, I noticed a line item for 10 hours of "research" on employment law in my state by an associate. I challenged this fee. I told my attorney I hired him because of his experience, so why was I paying him to have a junior associate research the law? To his credit, the lawyer removed the fee. But it should serve as a reminder that you need to be aware of the different ways lawyers might try to increase their billable hours.

The second inherent factor of the job that may conflict with your goals is risk aversion. By definition, lawyers tend to be risk-averse. Their aim is to minimize risk by adding language, conditions, and clauses to safeguard their clients. As a client, you might see this as a positive. However, there comes a point where the returns diminish. Eventually, as a CEO, you'll reach a level of acceptable risk, and it's time to stop pushing the issue (and racking up those mounting attorney fees). Your lawyer will never tell you that you've reduced risk "enough." That's your responsibility.

In short, an attorney plays a vital role in closing a deal after negotiations. But when working with that attorney, it's helpful to understand what motivates them while ensuring your needs are met—without paying more than necessary.

REAL LIFE NEGOTIATION—JIM: I've found a more effective way to use my lawyers' strengths. Instead of asking for permission, I tell them what I plan to do. Then, I ask for their help to ensure everything remains legal and our risks are minimized. In other words: "How can we do what I want without getting into trouble?" Alternatively, "How can we do what I want and minimize the risks?"

See what I did there? I removed the question of acting from the equation and shifted focus to ensure the lawyer thoroughly reviews the action we'll take. It's a way to involve your lawyers in creative risk management, which leads to a better outcome. As most lawyers are risk adverse, asking if something should happen opens the door for them to find a dozen reasons why it should not.

POP THE CHAMPAGNE

Negotiation isn't a one-time event; it's a cycle. How you handle the aftermath effects your readiness for the next round.

A deal isn't finished when it's signed. It's finished when it's implemented smoothly, both parties uphold their end of the bargain, and when the results speak for themselves. That's why documenting agreements, choosing the right legal advisors, and planning for contingencies like a potential breakup aren't just legal formalities—they're strategic tools.

And once the dust settles, don't forget to debrief. Take time to reflect on what worked, what didn't, and what you'd do differently next time because there will be a next time. Great negotiators treat every deal as practice for the next, constantly sharpening their skills.

So yes, pop the champagne. But while you're at it, open your notebook too. The next deal is already waiting.

〉 CHAPTER SIX TAKEAWAYS 〈

1. **Follow-through is everything.** Great negotiators don't just close—they ensure execution, address issues, and manage expectations post-deal.

2. **Debrief every deal.** Reflecting on what worked (and what didn't) sharpens your edge for the next negotiation.

3. **Keep momentum alive.** Use your credibility from this deal to seed the next opportunity—reputation compounds.

BRINGING IT ALL TOGETHER

YOU'VE NOW SEEN THE complete arc of negotiation—from how to prepare, to how to succeed under pressure, to what happens after the deal (or when it falls apart), and finally, how to maintain success over the long term.

You've observed two very different negotiators—Jim, the analytical strategist, and Onyi, the instinctive tactician—navigate real-world deals, share stories from the field, and demonstrate that there's no single "right" way to negotiate. The goal isn't to pick between their styles. It's to grasp the underlying principles and build your own confident, repeatable approach.

So, whether you're at the start of your next big deal, in the middle of a messy one, or recovering from a breakdown, you have the tools to:

- Prepare with purpose
- Adapt with agility
- Execute with clarity
- Follow through with strength
- And build long-term momentum that keeps you in control

Negotiation is a skill you develop—not a fixed personality trait. The more you practice, reflect, and adapt, the more influence you gain in every conversation. Now go out there and lead the next one with clarity, confidence, and control. Keep learning. Keep improving. Keep showing up.

We'll see you at the negotiating table.

ABOUT THE AUTHORS

DR. JIM SCHLECKSER

Dr. Jim Schleckser is a seasoned strategic advisor, bestselling author, and the head of The CEO Project—a peer-group program focused on helping CEOs double and triple their growth through disciplined advice and accountability systems.

With over thirty years of leadership experience in business strategy, technology, organizational development, process improvement, mergers & acquisitions, and sales & marketing, he has helped high-growth companies in both the public and private sectors reach new levels—across more than 42 countries. He has negotiated hundreds of licenses, agreements, and company sales during that time.

Jim holds a doctorate in Business Administration from the University of Maryland Global Campus, an MBA from the University of Connecticut, and a degree in Chemical Engineering from the University of Delaware. He is also a certified sommelier with the Guild of Master Sommeliers and has advanced credentials from the Wine & Spirits Education Trust. Jim's insights often appear in outlets like *The New York Times*, *Time*, HuffPost, NPR, and Inc.com, and his books—including *Great CEOs Are Lazy* and *Professional Drinking*—are translated into multiple languages.

Outside the boardroom, he's a dedicated soccer player, passionate reader, outdoorsman, and wine enthusiast—currently living in Potomac, Maryland.

You can contact Jim at jimschleckser@theceoproject.com or check out his website: www.TheCEOProject.com.

ONYI ODUNUKWE

Onyi Odunukwe is a self-made entrepreneur, investor, and deal architect known for structuring win–win deals that close and cash flow. Over the past decade, he's turned small negotiations into multi-million-dollar opportunities across construction, real estate, lending, media, and franchising.

By his mid-30s, he'd built a national construction company, a commercial lending firm, and stakes in 15+ businesses, along with dozens of commercial and residential developments acquired since 2020—compounding his net worth in under seven years.

His journey began at the University of Arkansas, where he launched Mr. O's Nutrition. A former Mr. Arkansas bodybuilder, he learned that repetition, observation, and leverage beat raw talent. Spotting inefficiencies in a nearby tanning model led to an offer that became one of his portfolio's top brands.

He helped scale Glo Tanning into one of the fastest-growing

U.S. franchises—ranked in Entrepreneur's Top 100 in 2025—using systems and negotiations he later applied to acquisitions, new ventures, and high-performing partnerships.

Committed to mentorship, Onyi believes great deals create value for all sides and that generosity and strategy are multipliers. "All my best ideas are stolen," he says—crediting disciplined learning and listening for "overnight" success.

Today, he continues to build, invest, and teach smart negotiation—showing entrepreneurs and operators how to turn knowledge into leverage and leverage into lasting wealth.

You can contact Onyi at onyi@odunukweventures.com or check out his website: www.odunukweventures.com.

www.ingramcontent.com/pod-product-compliance
Lightning Source LLC
Chambersburg PA
CBHW021326060726
47591CB00006B/1886